H(
MEDICAL SCHOOL
INTERVIEWS

HOW TO ACE YOUR
MEDICAL SCHOOL
INTERVIEWS:

224 Sample Questions and Answers with Insight on the Interviews and Premed Process

SAL EKTMI

Rev. date: 06/06/2013

To order additional copies of this book, contact:
Xlibris Corporation
1-888-795-4274
www.Xlibris.com
Orders@Xlibris.com
131620

CONTENTS

A Student Who Was Accepted By Every Medical School
That Interviewed Him

INTRODUCTION

THE INTERVIEW IS one of the most important components of the medical school application. You will only get into a medical school if you do well on the interviews. Surprisingly, a lot of people barely prepare for their interviews because they are overconfident or feel there is nothing they can do. There is a lot you can do and a lot you should do. Every hour spent preparing for the interview is more valuable than any other hour spent trying to get into medical school. You spend tens of thousands of hours to improve your GPA. You can have a great GPA, but if you do not put in the necessary hundreds of hours for interview preparation, it is likely to all go to waste.

The first chapter of this book is organized into a list of questions and sample answers. The questions in this book are divided into categories, and within each category, the more prevalent and important questions come first. Understand that many of these questions and answers were created with my personal experiences in mind. Many of these will not be relevant to your story, but they should help you come up with ideas for the types of questions and answers that could come up in your interviews. Knowing that you have already thought of answers for almost any question your interviewer could ask you replaces your insecurity and anxiety with confidence and excitement. I thought of my interview answers as a bag of stories and thoughts; I just had to get good at presenting the right item out of the bag at the right time. This skill is essential because no matter how many questions you study, there are bound to be some that you are not quite prepared for. In such a case, you can reach into your bag and pull out the most appropriate item. Before getting good at using the items in your bag, you must first increase the number of items you have. The good news is these items already exist! You just have to dig them out of your memory; this book is your shovel!

HOW TO USE THIS BOOK

BEFORE READING THIS book, open a new Word document. After reading each question, decide if it is a question somebody could ask you. If it is, write it down in your own document and try to come up with your best answer. Then read my sample answer to see if it gives you any ideas or guidance. For some questions, you will probably have to sit down with an adviser or mentor and discuss what type of answer you should give. Write down your answer to that question in your Word document. I suggest having questions and answers in different colors. Whether or not you decide the question is relevant to your situation, try to come up with similar questions that you could be asked and do the same process. By the end of the questions and answers chapter of this book, you should have your personalized document of questions and answers. This will be very helpful as your prepare for your interviews. The following chapter consists of advice and insights about the medical school interview process; read it like a normal book and take notes on the tips that you find helpful. The last chapter of this book consists of general premed advice. If you are already essentially finished with your premed process, this will not be very helpful. Otherwise, I strongly recommend reading it and taking notes.

CHAPTER 1

The Questions

General/background

1. Tell me about yourself. What brings you here today?

I AM THE third of five siblings raised in Miami. My mom was born and raised in Cuba. Her dad escaped Cuba on a raft. My dad was born and raised in a Lebanese war zone. His dad and two of my cousins on his side also lived with us in Miami, so I grew up in a home with a lot of people and a lot of diversity. This developed my ability to relate and connect with people from all backgrounds. Also, because I come from a family of immigrants, I had the ideals of hard work and perseverance ingrained in me from a young age.

At the age of ten, I fell in love with football and made a commitment to myself to do everything in my power to play at the highest level. When I got to college, I was able to transfer the work ethic and intensity I had learned from football to my academics. This allowed me to excel academically and enjoy the learning process. In my sophomore year, I injured my back playing football and had to end my football career. The reason I bring up football is that it helped me develop into the person I am today. It taught me to work hard, to work in a team, to perform under pressure, and to persevere.

The fact that I was no longer playing football gave me more time and energy to explore my interests. I was loving my science and volunteer experiences, so I decided to explore my interest in medicine. I shadowed many physicians and was amazed at the impact they were able to make on people's lives. So this past summer, I went to the Dominican Republic to get more hands on experience.

I was amazed at the amount of need for medical help and the amount of good physicians can do. I also got to experience what it feels like to provide medical care for people in need. I remember in one clinic there was an AIDS patient who had a fracture of his tibia. The bone had been literally sticking out of his leg for over a year because nobody would operate on an undocumented man. While it was sad and frustrating that there was nothing I could do about his AIDS or his fracture, it still felt incredibly rewarding to be able to clean his wound, redo his bandages, and connect with him on a personal level. I loved the work we did in the Dominican. I remember at the end of the long, hot clinics, everybody was excited to pack up and go home, but I wanted to stay and keep working.

Also, both my parents are physicians, so I know the lifestyle and work ethic necessary to practice medicine; so I know what I am getting myself into, and I am completely sure that this is what I want to do. So I just thank you for taking the time to interview me!

(Sometimes the interviewer interrupted me to ask questions on a part of my story. I would address the question but eventually try to work back into continuing my story. After I had given such a broad answer, the rest of the interview usually focused on talking about some aspects of my story.)

2. Why do you want to be a physician? What are you passionate about? What is your cause? How have you explored your desire to become a physician? What have you done to prepare yourself to be a physician?

I am fascinated by medicine; I believe it is the ultimate way to make a difference in the lives of others. I have shadowed many physicians and am amazed at the impact that they were able to make in people's lives, so this summer I went to the Dominican Republic to get more hands-on experience.

I was amazed at the amount of need for medical care and the amount of good physicians could do. In a clinic in a Haitian refugee camp, there was a young boy who had a burn scar behind his knee that did not allow him to straighten his leg. His peers called him "crab boy" because he walked on his hands and feet like a crab. Also, he could not attend school or anything. The physicians found a surgeon who was willing to do an operation and therapy for free. They gave the kid a chance to live a normal life. I was not able to have as big an impact as these physicians did, but I hope to be able to.

I was able to experience what it feels like to treat people in need. I remember in one clinic there was an AIDS patient who had a fracture of his tibia. The bone had been literally sticking out of his leg for over a year because nobody would operate on an undocumented man. While it was sad and frustrating that there was nothing I could do abut his AIDS or his fracture, it still felt incredibly rewarding to be able to clean his wound, redo his bandages, and connect with him on a personal level. I loved the work we did in the Dominican. I remember at the end of the long, hot clinics, everybody was excited to pack up and go home, but I wanted to stay and keep working.

Also, I love science and research, but science alone does not provide that deep human connection that is so important to me. I believe medicine is the ultimate balance between science and humanitarianism, and as a physician, I plan to do research that will have a far-reaching, long-lasting impact.

Also, both my parents are physicians, so I know the lifestyle and work ethic necessary to practice medicine; so I know what I am getting myself into, and I am completely sure that this is what I want to do. So I just thank you for taking the time to interview me!

3. Is there anything else you would like to tell me? What is the most interesting thing about you? Tell me something about you that I cannot get from your application.

(If I had not talked about my background yet, I would give this answer.) I would like to give you more background about who I am. I am the third of five kids raised in Miami. My mom was born and raised in Cuba; her dad escaped Cuba on a raft. My dad was born and raised in a Lebanese war zone. His dad and two of my cousins from Lebanon lived with us in Miami for many years, so I grew up in a home with a lot of people and a diverse culture. For example, Thanksgiving dinner at my house usually consists of over fifty people from Canada, Cuba, the Dominican Republic, Italy, Lebanon, Armenia, and the Philippines, and religions including Christian, Jewish, and Muslim.

(If I had already talked about that, I would give this answer.) I would like to tell you a story that gives a good picture of who I am.

This past spring break, when I stayed in school to study for my MCAT, I got a call from my pastor, who said that they were having a father-son lock-in at the church to allow for bonding but that one of the kids had no father figure in his life. He said there was nobody who could step in because everybody had left the campus for spring break, so he wanted me to spend twenty-four hours with this kid I had never met before. Initially, I thought I did not have time for this because I needed to improve my MCAT score, but I decided that playing as a father figure to that kid was more important, so I did it. I do not know if that extra day of studying would have improved my score, but I know that kid and his mom really appreciated what I did. This is the type of person I am.

4.   Why should we choose you out of all the other applicants? Convince me you would be a good physician. How do you feel your particular experiences, interests, and passions will add to the strength and diversity of the class and, ultimately, to the field of medicine?

Although there are other applicants with similar GPA and test scores as mine, there are very few of them who have done it while playing varsity division 1-A football. However, I believe that besides that, you should accept me because of my ability to connect with people from all backgrounds and my ability to work in teams. Because I grew up in a very large Cuban and Lebanese family, with blood relatives of different nationalities and religions from all over the world, I developed the ability to relate and connect with people from all different cultural backgrounds. Making these types of connection is very important to being a good physician. Also, playing football for nine seasons taught me how to work in teams. Being the captain of my high school football team taught me how to be a leader, and being a role player on my college football team taught me how to do whatever it takes to help the team win, even if it means setting somebody else up to make the play. This ability is extremely important in modern medicine because of all the collaboration that occurs in the clinical and research worlds. Sometimes a physician is the head surgeon of a large operation, and he needs to know how to be a leader. Sometimes a physician is a resident in an emergency situation, and he has to be comfortable taking orders, communicating, and doing whatever it takes to help the team win. I believe those skills will set me apart from the crowd.

5. What are your goals? What do you plan on doing ten or twenty years from now? What specialty are you considering? Are there any areas of medicine that are of particular interest to you?

Right now, my primary goal is to be accepted into medical school. Once I enroll in medical school, my primary goal will be to be the best physician possible. I am not sure what specialty what I want to go into, but I have shadowed many surgeons and loved what I saw, especially orthopedics. However, I have not seen everything, and I want to go into every clinical rotation thinking that it could be my specialty. As far as practice scenario is concerned, I see myself working in academic medicine because in addition to seeing patients, I want to be able to teach and conduct meaningful research. I do not know what type of research I will go into because so far I have loved all of my research experiences. However, I am fascinated with genetics and believe that it will be the source of many major advancements in the coming decades, so I could definitely see myself doing that.

6. In what type of practice scenario do you see yourself in the future? Why do you think you are suited for this particular scenario?

I am particularly suited for academic medicine because I love the collaboration, I have a passion for education and research, and I want to be able to focus on patient care, without the distractions of working in private practice.

I have tutored middle school students and younger premed students, including my younger sister. I love teaching and believe I am a good teacher because I take complex ideas and present them in their most basic forms before adding more details. Many of my professors at ___ are so passionate about what they teach that they make the learning process incredibly fun and exciting. They are also readily available to meet with me and seem to be truly invested in my understanding of the material. This is what has allowed me to excel in the classroom and gain a passion for education. I am excited to one day be able to pass this feeling on to my students.

I loved my research experiences in cellular biology, biochemistry, and parasitology. I plan to get involved in many research projects but am particularly excited about genetics research. Genetics is the future of medicine because it will allow us to have more personalized preventative medicine and care. I am excited about the possibility of being involved in the groundbreaking genetics research that will occur in the near future.

7.   If someone fifteen years from now were to write a book about you, what would you want to have included in that book?

(I would start by giving the answer to "Where do you see yourself in twenty years?" and then say this.) I hope to have made a significant contribution to the field of medicine by then. I would want the author to say that I am sincere, compassionate, hardworking, affable, and humble.

8.   Is there anything about medicine that scares you? What part of medicine do you like the least? If you could change one thing about the medical profession, what would it be? What is the biggest problem in health care? What do you think is the most pressing problem medicine is facing today? Can you think of any solutions?

The fact that we do not have a cure for everyone is the biggest problem, and the solution is to continue to conduct research. The part of medicine that I like the least is the idea of telling people that there is nothing we can do to help them. Although this would be a very sad situation, I would feel privileged to be in a position to support someone through the challenging times and to provide them with the best options and care possible.

For example, while I was working in a medical mission this summer, there was an AIDS patient who had had a severe leg fracture for over a year. Nobody would operate on him because he did not have papers. It was frustrating and sad that there was nothing I could do about his HIV or his fracture. However, I felt privileged to be able to clean his wound, redo his bandages, and connect with him on a personal level. This experience was sad, but it was also rewarding.

9.   Tell me the most altruistic thing you have done.

I have done a lot of volunteer work, but these had all been planned for, and none of them have been of a great inconvenience or cost to me. The one act that I did that was this past spring break, when I stayed at school to study for my MCAT. I got a call from my pastor, who said that they were having a father-son lock-in at the church to allow for bonding but that one of the kids had no father figure in his life. He said there was nobody who could step in because everybody had left the campus for spring break, so he wanted me to spend twenty-four hours with this kid I had never met before. Initially, I thought I did not have time for this because I needed to improve my MCAT score; but I decided that playing as a father figure to that kid was more important, so I did it. I do not know if that extra day of studying would have improved my score, but I know that kid and his mom really appreciated what I did. This is the type of person that I am.

10.   Have you always wanted to go into medicine?

I have always been interested in medicine, and I knew I wanted to do something involving science, but it was not until I got to college that I deeply began exploring my interest in medicine. I know how much of a commitment it is to study and practice, so I wanted to be completely sure this is for me before deciding to do it.

11.   How do you want me to remember you? What do you want me to tell the committee about you?

Primarily, I want you to remember me as the person that gave you very honest, sincere answers to all of your questions. I would also like you to remember me as someone that has have clearly studied the field of medicine and cemented his commitment to becoming a physician. Also, that I have the integrity, honesty, and physical and mental strength necessary to become a physician.

12.   What is that something that you do not like about yourself? What is your biggest weakness?

When I find something I am passionate about, I tend to allow it to take over my life. For example, in high school, my deepest passion was football. I trained so regularly for football that my academics suffered. In college, in addition to football, I became passionate about my academics and my desire to get accepted into medical school. I worked so hard and did my best in all of these areas that my social life suffered. I missed out on a lot of college experiences, and I know that my siblings and most of my friends had more memorable experiences in college than I did.

However, I have been working on improving this. For example, this past spring break, when I stayed at the school to study for my MCAT, I got a call from my pastor, who said that they were having a father-son lock-in at the church to allow for bonding but that one of the kids had no father figure in his life. He said there was nobody who could step in because everybody had left the campus for spring break, so he wanted me to spend twenty-four hours with this kid, whom I had never met before. Initially, I thought I didn't have time for it because I needed to improve my MCAT score, but I decided that playing as a father figure to that kid was more important, so I did it. I don't know if that extra day of studying would have improved my score, but I know that kid really appreciated what I did.

13. When was the last time you did something you regret? What is the biggest mistake you have made?

The last significant thing I regret doing was continuing to practice football while my back was seriously injured. I was so determined to play that I did not allow myself to believe that I was seriously hurt. I also did not want to let my teammates down. This caused my injury to get to the point where I had to end my football career. I learned that perseverance is great, but it must be taken with a dose of wisdom. Also, the fact that I was no longer playing football opened many opportunities for me.

14. What was the most stressful event in your life? How did you handle it? What is the most important event that has happened to you in the last five years? What is the worst thing that has ever happened to you? Tell me about a tough decision you made.

The most stressful event of my life was deciding to end my football career. I had such a deep desire to continue playing football at the collegiate level, and I had spent so many years training to be in the position I was in. I also did not want to let my teammates down. I knew that if I had continued my therapy, I would have been able to play at least one more season, but I would have jeopardized my health in the long term. I handled this situation by clearing my mind and focusing on the pros and cons of each option. It seems an easy decision now, but deciding to walk away from the game that helped me become the person I am today was an extremely stressful event. In addition to preserving my health in the long term, this decision provided me with more time and energy to explore ways in which I could make a significant impact on the lives of others. This led me to choose a career in medicine and allowed me to investigate and cement my commitment to medicine. I believe that I handled this situation in the best way possible.

15. So is medicine your backup plan now that your football career did not go as planned?

No. I was on the premed track before getting injured. If I had continued playing football, I would have probably taken a year off before applying for medical school because of the time commitments. However, it was only after getting injured that I had the time and energy to cement my convictions about going into medicine.

16. What are your best attributes?

I am hardworking, compassionate, and humble. My work ethic is demonstrated in my ability to play division 1 varsity football while maintaining a GPA above 3.9. Compassion and humility are more difficult to demonstrate verbally, but anybody who knows me will use these adjectives to describe me.

17. Tell me about your personal background.

I am the third of five kids raised in Miami. My mom was born and raised in Cuba; her dad escaped Cuba on a raft. My dad was born and raised in a Lebanese war zone. His dad and two of my cousins from Lebanon lived with us in Miami for many years, so I grew up in a home with a lot of people and a diverse culture. For example, Thanksgiving dinner at my house usually consists of over fifty people from Canada, Cuba, the Dominican Republic, Italy, Lebanon, Armenia, and the Philippines, and religions including Christian, Jewish, and Muslim. So you can imagine it was a culture shock when I left that diversity to move to North Carolina. Thankfully, I was able to make some great friends on the football team and the Organization of Latin American Students that really helped me integrate into the new culture and make North Carolina a second home.

18. Can you convince me that you can cope with the workload in medical school? What is the one thing that distinguishes you from the rest of the applicants?

Yes. I maintained a GPA above a 3.9 while playing division 1-A college football and doing extracurricular activities.

19. How would your friends describe you? What type of person are you?

My friends would primarily describe me as a faithful friend because I am always there for them in times of need. For example, one of my friends got arrested for public intoxication, and all my other friends decided to wait until the next morning to try to get him. I went straight to the jail, paid his bail, waited there for him until 5:00 a.m., and brought him to my house so that he could sleep. They would also tell you that I am hardworking, humble, compassionate, honest, and fun to be around.

20. How would you assess your skills in dealing with the public?

I am the third of five kids, who are very close in age, and have great relationships with all my siblings. This has taught me how to work in groups. I learned when and how to get my point across in a respectful way, even when everybody in the group has a different opinion. I have such a great relationship with my younger sister that she chose to go to the same university as me, even though she was accepted at higher-ranked schools.

Also, growing up in a home with so much cultural diversity allowed me to gain an appreciation for different cultures and connect with people from all different cultures.

While playing high school football, I built great relationships with all my teammates and was elected captain during my last two seasons. I had to relate with everybody to get them all on the same page. I also built strong relationships with all my teammates in college. My relationship with almost all of them has stayed strong, even after I had stopped playing for almost two years.

21. Give evidence that you relate well with others.

While volunteering at a camp for children with chronic skin conditions last summer, I had the privilege of meeting ___, an eight-year-old boy who had eczema and autism. When we first met, he basically ignored me and barely spoke to anybody; his disability made it difficult for him to make friends. I made a constant effort to get to know him and eventually discovered that he had an enthusiasm for drawing pictures of zombies. Later, when it was time for the talent show, my connection with him allowed me to help him overcome his fear of being onstage. Just before the start of the show, he learned the moves and danced fantastically onstage in front of everybody. This really helped him come out of his shell. On the last day, he was singing, dancing, and explaining each of his countless zombie pictures in detail to his new friends.

22. Why do *you* want to help people?

It is in my nature; helping people brings me much more satisfaction than being self-centered. This comes partly as a response to my upbringing. I was raised in a materialistic, self-centered society in Miami, and there was a constant pressure to be dragged into that lifestyle and way of thinking. However, I quickly discovered that only leads to emptiness and dissatisfaction, especially when compared to the amazing feeling of helping people in need. Medicine is definitely the best way to help people in need.

23. In your personal statement/essay, what diagnosis did that person have? What was the diagnosis for your back injury? Why did it not heal completely?

24. Why did you have a low score on MCAT verbal reasoning?

I spent equal amount of time studying each subject and was disappointed in my verbal score. However, I hope that my 4.0 scores in my English and humanities courses show that I am able to read complex material and think critically.

Ethical and situational

**I got far fewer ethical questions (maybe three) than did all of my friends. I believe this was because I determined the direction of my interview. I was open to talking about my experiences, so most of the interviews focused on those experiences. This was great because that was what I was most comfortable talking about. My mom used to interview medical students, and she said she would only ask ethical questions if the interview was stalling. If the interviewee was opening up and giving a good idea of who they are, there would be no need to interrupt that with a hypothetical question; the point of the interview is for them to get to know who you are.

Remember, hypothetical questions are not looking for your opinion; they want to know your process.

If you ever need a moment to concentrate, ask for it. Never look up or away without first asking for a second to concentrate.

If they ask you a question that you cannot think of an answer for, follow this procedure:

1. "Wow, that is an interesting question. Can you give me a second to think about it?"
2. Change the question to one you can answer.
3. "I should know this, but I don't, and I will find out."

If you have an ethics question where your answers seem wrong, say, "I would consult the legal department of the hospital so they could assess what the American Medical Association recommends in this situation."

25. Would you ever lie to a patient?

I would never lie to a patient about something medical, but small lies can have harmless benefits. For example, if I am seeing an elderly woman for a hand injury, and she asks me how she looks, and she looks noticeably worse than the last time I saw her, I would still tell her that she looks good. This is a harmless lie that boosts the patient's confidence and avoids an unnecessary awkward situation.

26. If there was a virus pandemic that was highly contagious, would you, as a healthy medical professional, go to work and risk getting sick?

Many professions have risks, and I understand that medicine is one of them. I would not run away from my responsibilities because this would be when I would be most needed. We would have to figure out a way to treat people without getting infected. We might even have to wear a full-body suit to avoid any direct contact.

27. What do you think about a physician who does not want to do a risky operation on an AIDS patient for fear of being infected?

I try to make it a point not to judge other people's decisions, but I can tell you what I would do in that situation. I would take whatever precautions are available and do the procedure because, as a physician, I have a responsibility to help patients. All careers have risks, and I am willing to take those risks to care for people in need.

28. Should expense be considered when treating someone with a small chance of survival?

Well, first, we have to ask the question if cost should be considered at all. To some extent, it should because we do not want to burden the system or the patient with tests and procedures that are not going to improve the quality of care.

In theory, we would want to say that there are limited resources, so we should allocate them to the people with the greatest chance of recovering. However, in practice, it does not really make sense because that would be asking physicians to play God. Physicians should not be in a position to decide who gets to live and who does not. It is the physician's responsibility to provide hope, not take it away.

Several studies have indicated that up to 30 percent of what we spend on medicine does not improve the quality of care, so if we are going to conserve resources, we should focus on those costs that are not improving care, not costs that are saving lives and providing hope.

29. If a patient was dying from bleeding, would you transfuse blood if you knew they would not approve for religious reasons?

I would first make sure they understood that if they refused the transfusion, they would run a high risk of dying. If they understood that and still did not want the transfusion, I would not do the transfusion. It would be heartbreaking to let somebody die, knowing that I could have saved them, but I have to respect their choice.

30. If a class got canceled, and you suddenly had a three-hour gap between classes, what would you do?

I would go to the library and study. Being a student-athlete taught me to adopt the philosophy that every waking moment should be used to do something productive.

31. You are taking a final exam and notice there is a student cheating. What would you do?

This happened to me before. I do not think it is my role to play proctor or authority figure, so I would not do anything. I know that I have studied for this exam, so I will do well without cheating.

32. There is a lot of multidisciplinary collaboration in the medical field today. What would you do if you were the head physician on a team and a nurse or social worker was trying to command the operation?

I would make sure to talk to them on a one-on-one setting to make sure they do not think I am trying to put them in their place in front of a group. I would respectfully remind them that the team works best when they play a certain role, and I would ask them to focus on that role.

33. What would you do about problems with alcohol and obesity in the United States?

I would increase awareness on the serious health hazards of being obese or alcoholic and how they can both be prevented and treated.

34. How would you calm a nervous patient?

I would reassure them that I know what I am doing, that I am there to support them, and that I have their best interest in mind. It is difficult to explain how to do it, but when I have compassion for somebody, it shows. Once the patient sees that I am invested in their situation, they would probably be more willing to trust me.

35. What do you think about TV and print ads on prescription drugs?

I like that it increases awareness and question asking. If the patient does not need the drug, it is the physician's role to not provide the prescription.

36. Should doctors be allowed to "pull the plug" on terminally ill patients? How do you feel about playing God? What if there is a disagreement among family members on what should be done?

Patients should have the right to refuse further treatment at any time. If the patient is unable to express what he would want done, then it is our responsibility to determine what he would want, either through his will or through his next of kin. If the family cannot agree on what the patient would have done, I would urge them to come to an agreement, considering what the patient would want, not what they want.

37. If somebody stole your idea and presented it as their own, what would you do?

I would first talk to them about it. If that does not work, I would find out what my rights are and speak to an authority figure.

38. How do you help people who do not want to be helped? How do you know when you have done enough and need to step back?

I would comfort them and make it clear that I have their best interest in mind. I would explain the benefits of being helped. I would not step back until the person made it clear that they reject my effort to help and are unwilling to listen to what I have to say. In that case, I would tell them, "You have the freedom to do as you wish, but just know that I am here to help you, and I have your best interest in mind. I cannot help you if you do not let me, so as soon as you decide that you are going to let me help you, please contact me and I will be there for you."

39. What do you do to a patient or a patient's family member who does not understand what is going on?

It is important to understand the circumstances and respond accordingly. Do they not understand what is going on because of lack of education, lack of fluency in English or Spanish, or some other reason? If it is due to a language barrier, I would make sure to find somebody that speaks their language. If it is due to lack of education, I would explain the situation in its most basic form and even draw what I am talking about if necessary. It is very important for me to make sure the patient knows what is going on and is making decisions for themselves because I have been on the other side of that conversation. After doing months of rehab to try to make it back to spring football practice, the orthopedist sat me down and said that he could clear me to play but that I needed to understand the implications of the decision I was making. He explained the risks of continuing to play, and that allowed me to make the best decision. He seemed invested in my situation but allowed me to make the decision for myself. I want to be able to do the same for my patients.

40. What would you do if you caught your roommate cheating on his AMCAS application?

I would talk to him about it and try to convince him that he could get accepted without cheating. If he disagreed, I would advise him to spend a year improving his application so that he could reapply next year and get in.

41. What do you think about condoms being distributed in high schools?

I love it. I do not think that handing out condoms is going to make children any more promiscuous. It will increase awareness, and people will make it a habit to have safe sex. Condoms should be handed out in addition to adequate sexual education.

42. Would you transfuse blood to the child of a Jehovah's Witness?

Yes. In order to give informed consent, a patient must have competence, adequate information, freedom from coercion. If the child does not have these, I believe that giving them treatment gives them more freedom. If the church has a problem with it, we can discuss that after the fact, but in an emergency situation, I will save the child's life.

43. What sorts of ethical problems can you see coming up in the medical profession?

The advancement in technology and understanding of human genetics will definitely be a source of ethical debate. For example, if we get to the point where a couple can choose some of the physical and mental characteristics of their children, we must discuss if that should be allowed. On one hand, it would increase the productivity of the human race; but on the other, it would be interfering with nature. It would also provide another advantage to upper-class families that lower-income families cannot afford.

44. How would you deal with a patient who is in pain?

It depends on what type of pain we are talking about. If it is serious postsurgery type of pain, then I would prescribe them a serious painkiller. If somebody just walks into the clinic and claims to be in pain, I would try to figure out what is causing the pain and respond accordingly. That may require prescription of a certain medication, emotional or psychological support, or some combination of those.

45. What would you do if your patient's family became very emotional about the diagnosis and began blaming it on you?

I know that their being upset has nothing to do with the quality of care that I am providing. I understand that finding out a loved one is sick can bring out a lot of emotions that are difficult to control. I would first let them calm down and make sure they have water. I would then do everything in my power to make it clear to them that I know what I am doing and that I have the patient's best interest in mind. I would also make sure that they understand what is going on.

46. Do you think scientific information should ever be withheld from publication?

This is science; we should not censor anything. When we do that, the terrorists have won. There are huge benefits to doing this research that humanity needs to benefit from. An infectious virus would be a poor choice for a bioweapon anyways because it would spread across the world in a matter of days.

47. What are your thoughts on using fetal tissue for research or disease treatment?

There are currently no diseases that can be treated with fetal tissue. If that becomes an option in the future, I would support it as long as the tissues are obtained in an ethical manner, such as by obtaining it from an abortion clinic. As long as we are not taking fetuses that would have otherwise been born, then we should use them to help treat people that already exist. I support using it for research because that is the only way to get to a new treatment.

48. What are your thoughts on embryonic stem cell research or using embryonic stem cells to treat diseases?

Well, adult stem cells actually have many of the same treatment possibilities as embryonic stem cells. However, if a certain research or treatment requires embryonic stem cells, I support it, as long as the fetal tissue is obtained in ethically acceptable ways.

49. What are your thoughts about abortion?

It is a tough issue. On one hand, we want to protect all human life in any form. On the other hand, we would be giving the government too much control by allowing them to tell women what to do with their bodies, especially in cases of rape. Also, if abortion were illegal, it would be difficult to enforce, and there would soon be underground networks of unskilled abortionists. This would be detrimental to women's health and defeat the purpose of the ban. So while I can see both sides of the issue, I lean to being pro-choice.

50. If you were an abortionist and an underage girl asked you for an abortion, and she did not want to tell her parents, what would you do?

I would first try to get her to tell her parents. If that were not an option, I would advise her to try to get a judge to give her legal authority to make the decision for herself. Otherwise, I would not do it because it is illegal.

51. Do you believe that physician-assisted death should be legalized?

Patients should always have the right to refuse treatment at any time, but the question of lethal medications is much more challenging. Many patients want to have control over when they die and often feel that their lives are not worth living once they are in very critical conditions. In theory, it does not harm anybody, but this would be asking physicians to take life away from their patients. That is the opposite of what physicians work for, so I am against allowing physicians to assist patients in suicide.

52. A sixty-eight-year-old married woman has a newly discovered cancer. Her life expectancy is six months. How would you inform her?

I believe it is the physician's duty to provide hope. I would research the literature in order to give her the percentage of people that live past six months. I would also find out what new studies and potential therapies are being researched for that type of cancer. I would then inform her that she has a malignant tumor in the late stages and tell her the chances of surviving past six months. I would tell her what our options are, as well as what new studies are being done on that type of cancer. I would tell her that I am there to support her. I would be encouraging, without providing blind optimism. I would then listen to what the patient has to say and respond accordingly.

53. A thirty-four-year-old man presents with AIDS and tells you, as his physician, that he does not want to tell his wife. What would you do?

I would explain to him that he would most likely transmit the virus to her. I would tell him that he has an obligation to society and to his wife to tell her. I would let him know that I would help him receive any psychological help necessary and would be willing to be in the room once he told her. If he still refused, I would treat him, try to quickly earn his trust, and convince him to tell her.

54.   A sixteen-year-old patient tells you that she wants birth control but does not want to tell her parents. What would you do?

I would explain to her the risks involved with sex, besides pregnancy. I would also make sure that she is sexually active because she wants to be, not because she feels pressured. I would tell her the risks and effects of taking birth control. I would strongly advise her to tell her parents. Although I would not want to encourage her sexual activity, I would prescribe her birth control because not prescribing it is not going to alter her sexual activity or her relationship with her parents.

55.   If you could find a cure for cancer or AIDS, which would it be?

I would find a cure for cancer because it affects more people, and we do not know entirely how to prevent it.

56.   What if you had a patient that did not pay?

I do not like to think of a patient as a client. I want to be a physician, not a businessman. This is part of the reason I want to work in an academic setting. I want to be able to treat patients without thinking about my income. If we are assuming that I am in private practice, I would have my staff find out why the patient did not pay. If it was because of lack of means, I would consider it charity.

57.   What would you do if a doctor gave you orders that you knew would harm the patient?

This is an interesting question because even when I "know I am right," I can still be wrong. Because I am a student of the doctor giving orders, he probably has a reason for giving that order.

With that considered, the answer to your question depends on the situation. If this was an emergency situation and the attending physician gave orders, we would function like the military—that is, we would act first and ask questions later. If this was not an emergency, I would tell him that I do not understand why he wants to do that. I would ask him to explain it to me. If he gave me an explanation that I knew was wrong, I would tell him that I do not feel comfortable doing that.

58. You see a patient who gives you some grief and complaints. At the end of treatment, he asks you if he was a good patient. What would you say?

The patient has the right to complain; it is his health we are talking about. There is no need to bring up a confrontation. As a physician, you want people to like you, and it is difficult for people to like you if they think that you do not like them. I would smile and say, "You are not always the easiest patient to work with, but I like you, and I enjoy the challenge."

59. Your supervising physician comes to work drunk. How would you handle the situation?

I would confront him directly and advise him to go home immediately. If he did not cooperate, I would inform somebody else who is in charge.

60. Is it ethical for doctors to strike?

Physicians have a duty to treat the sick. It is unethical to allow politics or money to interfere with that duty. Striking is not the best way to deal with complaints. We are all educated people. If we have a problem, we should open a formal discussion.

61. Should people have the right to sell their organs?

Organ selling is currently illegal in the United States for multiple reasons. It is morally questionable to sell parts of the human body. People who have enough money would probably be willing to spend it all to save their lives. This would make it incredibly difficult for the average person to afford an organ. It also might cause organ donors to demand compensation. This could decrease the number of organ donors and create an additional financial burden on our health system.

I believe legalization has some valid points. Organs are our property, so the government should not stop us from selling them. Also, in these difficult financial times, there may actually be a lot of people willing to sell their organs, and this might be the answer to the organ shortage. It is estimated that in America, if 0.06 percent of adults donated kidneys, the waiting list for organs would be fulfilled.

All things considered, I do not think legalizing organ sale is the best way to solve the organ donor problem. I would change the legislation so that we assume everybody wants to be an organ donor, unless they specifically say they do not want to be donors.

62.   Do you think marijuana should be legal for medical purposes? What about for recreational purposes?

For medicinal purposes, there are several clear reports that marijuana provides great benefits for certain patients. It should definitely be legalized for medicinal purposes.

I support the recreational legalization of marijuana for multiple reasons. The main reason is economic. If we started taxing marijuana sales instead of spending millions enforcing marijuana legislation, we could greatly improve our economic situation. It would also take a lot of money and power out of the hands of violent drug dealers. I also think that because marijuana users are already in the illegal drug-buying world, they are more likely to get into more serious drugs. Also, I think a lot of kids do marijuana because it is illegal and they want to be rebellious. Lastly, marijuana charges get a lot of good people into serious trouble with the law. I think it is only a matter of time before marijuana becomes legal for recreational use throughout the entire country.

63.   Do you think that there should be mandatory HIV testing for couples wanting to get married?

Maybe for people with multiple sex partners, enforced HIV testing would be cost-effective. However, for people wanting to get married, it would not be. It would be an overuse of the system and would do very little in preventing the spread of HIV. It is also a violation of privacy. I do not support this at all.

64. Would you prefer to provide less effective medicine to more people or more effective medicine to fewer people?

I would prefer to provide less effective medicine to more people because there are diminishing returns as we invest more on an individual patient. If we get everybody basic care, it could still be somewhat effective, especially if that care focuses on awareness, prevention, and early treatment.

Either way, I do not believe this is a decision we need to make. A recent study by the Dartmouth Institute for Health Policy suggests that 30 percent of what we spend on health care does not improve quality of care. If we eliminate unneeded care, there will be more than enough resources in our system to cover everybody.

65. If you won the lottery, what would you do with the money?

I would save enough to pay for medical school tuition, a decent house, and a decent car. I would donate the rest and the majority of what I earn the rest of my life to charity.

Political

**Make sure to stay up-to-date on the news. Be ready to talk about the latest controversial issues. I got the *USA Today* app on my phone and allowed it to send me push notifications.

66. How do you stay up-to-date on the news?

I have the *USA Today* app on my phone, and I have it set to send me push notifications whenever something important happens. I read the articles whenever something important happens, or whenever I scan my phone and I find something interesting.

67. What are the pros and cons of our health care system? (pre-Obamacare)

Pros: For people who have health insurance, the medical care is excellent. They generally get every relevant test to make sure that the physician is as well-informed as possible.

Cons: Not everybody has health insurance. A major reason for this is that it is so easy for physicians to be sued. This forces them to run many unnecessary tests and procedures that drive up the cost of medicine. This also results in a rise in malpractice insurance premiums, which leads to increased cost of medicine. There should be a board of physicians that would look at every case before it can be brought to court.

Another major issue with our health care system is that it is a disease care system; we often wait until people are seriously sick before intervening. If we focus on increasing awareness, prevention, and early treatment, we will improve the quality of care and reduce costs.

68. Which politicians are currently impacting medicine? Do you agree with the decisions they are making? What do you think about the recent changes to health care? (Obamacare)

President Barack Obama is definitely impacting medicine. There are some aspects of the Affordable Care Act that I like, some that I do not like, and some important issues that it does not address. I like that it aims to increase the number of people who have adequate health coverage and makes sure that insurance companies pay as much as is necessary to treat the patient. I like that it does not allow insurance companies to discriminate against people based on disease history.

However, currently, I do not think we can afford Obamacare; and if we attempt to install it, we will have to restrict patients' decisions and ration care. In the first twenty years of the plan, there is a proposed $3 trillion for Medicare alone. I also do not like the idea of government takeover of medicine. An individual patient and physician will be much more successful if they determine the best and most cost-effective treatment options for each specific situation than if they have a board of fifteen people thousands of miles away telling them what type of plan and care patients need.

Lastly, it does not address the malpractice suit problem. A major reason for the increased cost of medicine is that it is so easy for physicians to be sued. This forces them to run many unnecessary tests and procedures that drive up the costs of medicine. This also results in a rise in malpractice insurance premiums, which leads to increased cost of medicine. There should be a board of physicians that would look at every case before it can be brought to court.

69.   If you had the power, what changes would you make to our health care system?

I would first address the malpractice issue. It is too easy for physicians to be sued. This forces them to run many unnecessary tests and procedures that drive up the costs of medicine. This also results in a rise in malpractice insurance premiums, which leads to increased costs of medicine. There should be a board of physicians that would look at every case before it can be brought to court.

Another major issue with our health care system is that it is a disease care system; we often wait until people are seriously sick before intervening. If we focus on increasing awareness, prevention, and early treatment, we will improve the quality of care and reduce costs.

70.   Most people know that smoking cigarette is unhealthy, but they still do it; do you really think increasing awareness would get us anywhere?

There is still a lot we can do. For example, I believe the antitobacco advertisements that show people who have to speak from their necks are very effective. However, because they are on TV, they get registered as another ridiculous thing on TV that has no relevance to everyday life. If we could get more of those people to talk at schools, it would have more of an impact. It would teach kids that smoking is not cool and has real consequences. Preventing people from ever trying smoking is the best way to stop tobacco use. Also, a lot of people want to quit smoking but do not know how. If we increase awareness on how to quit smoking, more people will be able to quit. These solutions are far more cost-effective than just waiting until people develop cancer or cardiovascular disease.

71.   Name some strategies to address the problem of smoking among teens; talk about some that have not been tried before.

72.   What is your opinion of a national health insurance?

Although I like the idea of providing health care for everyone, I do not support this idea. With the current costs of medicine, it would be unaffordable. If we tried to install it, there would be more restrictions on patients' decisions and rationing of care. It would also be less organized.

I also do not like the idea of government takeover of medicine. An individual patient and physician will be much more successful if they determine the best and most cost-effective treatment options for each specific situation than if they have a board of fifteen people thousands of miles away telling them what type of plan and care patients need.

73. What do you think about the disadvantages and advantages of managed health care?

It lowers costs, but can restrict patients' decisions and lead to rationing of care.

74. Is Obamacare unconstitutional?

I see why some people believe that it is. However, it has to pay for the emergency medicine of uninsured people. If those people do not pay for their own coverage, then they need to be taxed for this service.

75. Who do you think is responsible for the rationing of health care?

The government is responsible for rationing health care because individuals and businesses tend to do what is in their best interest, not the best interest of the entire country.

76. What is the difference between Medicare and Medicaid?

They are both government-sponsored programs. Medicare is designed to help with long-term care for the elderly and disabled, while Medicaid covers health care costs for the poor.

77. What are HMOs and PPOs, and what is your opinion about them?

HMOs were designed to reduce health costs by reducing overutilization. HMOs require patients to select a primary physician, who can refer them to a specialist in the network, if necessary. It is a good money-saving device for a lot of people, but there are many rules and restrictions.

PPOs allow patients to choose their doctors and hospital from any that are in the network. PPOs are less restrictive because they allow patients to handle many aspects of their health care. For example, a patient can see a specialist directly without first visiting a primary physician. However, this can be far more expensive than an HMO.

78. Do doctors make too much money?

No. A doctor spends a minimum of ten years in education and training after high school, and many are in training for more than fifteen years. They are living on student loans and contributing nothing to their family's income for a long time. When a doctor emerges from training, he is usually over thirty years old and over $150,000 in debt. Doctors are fairly compensated for the hard work put in to become physicians and practice medicine and for the responsibility and stress they deal with every day. People do not choose a career in medicine to make money. Working that hard in almost any other professional occupation would result in more money.

79. What do you think of the priority system for organ recipients?

Many factors are taken into consideration: distance of transplant center from the donor hospital, blood type, medical urgency, wait time, donor size, and tissue type. I believe these should all be taken into account. I spent a lot of time researching this and could not find any source that says health and age of recipient are taken into account. If they are not, I would also add them to the list of things to be considered. I also believe that whether or not the recipient is an organ donor and a blood donor should have at least some effect on their place on the recipient list.

80. Give me a list of three political issues that are of great importance in the health care field.

   a. Obamacare
   b. Malpractice laws
   c. Spiraling cost of medicine

81. What would you do about the organ shortage problem?

I would make two major changes. I would make a change so that everybody donates their organs when they die, unless they request not to.

I would also make a change so that people who are organ donors have somewhat of an advantage when in need of receiving an organ.

82. What do you think about immigration reform?

I support Obama's movement to make it more difficult for illegal immigrants to get in to the United States, increase the number of visas that allow people to come here legally and eventually even become citizens, increase programs to legalize undocumented immigrants who are already here, and create programs to help immigrants adjust to life in the United States. Immigration is an essential part of this country. I come from a family of immigrants. However, we need to make sure it is not free for all to enter the country.

83. What do you think about affirmative action?

I support affirmative action, especially as it pertains to medical schools. We need more professionals that are capable of connecting with and understanding our diverse population. Some people say that this is giving minorities an unfair advantage. However, most minorities are already coming from disadvantaged backgrounds. There could be economic, social, educational, and even language barriers. Also, minorities do not tend to have the same professional connections as most other Americans.

84. Should the federal government reinstate the death penalty? Explain.

There have been multiple studies on the efficacy of the death penalty in reducing crime, and they usually come to different conclusions, so it is unclear if the death penalty affects the crime rate. It is morally controversial, and putting someone on the death penalty actually costs more than putting them in prison for life. This is because of all the legal work involved in keeping people on death row. I therefore see no reason to support the death penalty. If the system changes, or if we can find conclusive evidence that it does reduce crime, then there will have to be a new discussion.

85. What are the prospects for a lasting peace in South Africa? Eastern Europe? The former USSR? The Middle East?

I believe that the prospects of a long-lasting peace are slim. People are fueled by their greed, revenge, and ignorance of other cultures. However, I still believe that peace is possible, and we must strive for it.

86. What do you think about NAFTA?

Pros: Trade has increased drastically. Estimates are that NAFTA increases economic output in the United States by as much as 0.5 percent a year. Some service industries, such as health care and financial services, see an increase in exports. Farm products also reap the benefits of NAFTA's lower tariffs. U.S. consumers also benefit from NAFTA. Mexican oil can be imported for less, lowering the cost of gas in the United States and decreasing reliance on oil from the Middle East. Lower gas prices means food can be transported more cheaply as well.
Cons: NAFTA led to the loss of 500,000-750,000 jobs in the United States, thanks to companies moving across the border to Mexico. As a result, workers in those industries affected by NAFTA could not bargain for higher wages. NAFTA created negative consequences for Mexico too. It allowed government-subsidized U.S. farm products into Mexico, where local farmers could not compete. As Mexicans lost their farms, they went to work in substandard conditions.

Research

87A. Tell me about your research.

My major research project as an undergraduate was at the ___. We were looking for a way to increase cell survival rates in transplants. The cells had a low survival rate due to lack of oxygen until angiogenesis could occur. We were looking at a mouse model, and I was specifically looking at a myoblast cell line called C2C12. The mechanism I was exploring for increasing cell survival was the use of adenosine. Adenosine is believed to lower the metabolic rates of cells, so I was testing if it would increase cell survival in hypoxic conditions. I did all of the cell culture work, carried out the experiments, and helped analyze the data. We found that adenosine concentrations of up to 1 milimolar actually increased cell survival. The abstract was published, and the paper is still being finalized.

87B. How did you count the number of living cells?

We used an MTS assay. In viable cells, MTS compound is reduced to formazan by reductase enzymes. The absorbance at 490nm is directly related to formazan concentration, which is proportional to the number of living cells.

87C. How does adenosine lower the metabolic rate of cells?

It binds to G protein-coupled receptors. When adensoine binds, they couple to the Gi protein to inhibit adenylate cyclase activity. This lowers the cytoplasmic concentration of cAMP and, thus, lowers the metabolic rate.

87D. What are other researchers trying to do to address this problem? Why do you think your solution is better?

Several studies are exploring mechanisms to improve the vascularity of the recipient site. Vascular endothelial growth factor is a commonly researched option. I think it is important to research all possible treatments. However, I believe that reducing the metabolic demands of the transplant is a simpler and less invasive option than altering the recipient site.

88. How is your research clinically useful?

Stem cell transplant is currently used to treat many forms of hematologic cancer. Also retinal cell transplants are used to tread eye circuitry diseases. Research is also being done on the role of cell transplants to treat diabetes and Parkinson's disease. However, for any of these treatments to be successful, the cells must have a high survival rate. Knowing that I contributed to something that could potentially benefit all these treatments is a great feeling.

89. How would you describe the relationship between science and medicine?

Medicine is a science and an art. It focuses on the ways to prevent and treat diseases through a holistic humanistic approach, while science focuses on what actually occurs at the molecular and cellular level. Both approaches rely primarily on observation. They each help support the other.

For example, the war on cancer led by Nixon did not cure cancer, but it provided a much better understanding of cellular processes. More recently, understanding of these processes has allowed for many forms of cancers to be treated. Conversely, Edward Jenner used a medical observation (the fact that cowpox prevents smallpox) that led to the discovery of vaccinations. This discovery led to a better understanding of antibodies and the immune system.

I love science, research, and learning. I just completed a microsurgery training course that I loved. I have really enjoyed the research I have done in biology and chemistry labs, but science on its own does not provide me with that deep human connection that is so important to me. I believe medicine is the ultimate balance between science and humanitarianism. I also believe that medical research allows for a more far-reaching and long-lasting impact.

90A. Tell me about your parasitology research.

I received a research grant from my university to explore the relationship between infection with protozoan parasites and anthropomorphic indicators of malnutrition.

90B. What species of parasites were you researching?

90C. How does parasitic infection lead to malnutrition?

91A. Tell me about your chemistry research.

The lab I was working in developed an antitumor drug that binds to the DNA of cancerous cells, inducing apoptosis. My job was to react the DNA with the drug, use anion-exchange chromatography to separate the reacted DNA and drug from the rest of the mixture, analyze the purity, and use uv/vis spectroscopy to analyze the concentration.

91B. How does anion-exchange chromatography work?

91C. How does the drug differentiate between cancerous and noncancerous cells?

It does not.

91D. How do you know when the DNA has fully reacted?

91E. How do you know which peak to collect?

91F. How do you determine the concentration and the purity?

92A. Tell me about the work you are doing now at ___ hospital.

I am doing tissue engineering on mice in the plastic surgery department under Dr. ___. We are focusing on the low retention rates of autologous fat grafts. We believe this is because unvascularized fat must receive nutrients through diffusion, and thinker grafts experience central necrosis because of their low SA:V ratio.

The main surgeon created an external volume expansion vacuum bra that he uses on patients before fat grafting. The idea is that the bra induces angiogenesis and increases the volume of the breast so that thin layers of fat can be diffusely microinjected into the tissue. Although he has done this procedure on over a thousand patients and gotten great results, the basic science behind it has not yet been proven in a lab. He created an external volume expander for the dorsum of mice and received a grant to see if it induces cell proliferation and angiogenesis and allows more fat to be grafted into the tissue.

That experiment will not begin until March, so in the meantime, I am writing a review article on the role of the recipient site in fat grafting. I have microsurgery experience with rats, but I am working on improving my skills with mice so I can be more useful when the fat grafting experiments actually begin.

92B. Where does the fat come from in the mice studies?

93. Where was your abstract/paper published?

94. Tell me about your early scientific motivation.

For my fourth-grade science fair project, I looked at the effect of music genre on crossword puzzle completion speed. It was so much fun to conduct the study, analyze the data, and present it at the science fair that I knew I wanted a career involving science. When I got to college, my scientific curiosity really flourished, cementing my convictions about science.

95. What major advancement has medicine made over the past ten years? What do you think is the future of medicine? From which field will the next major advancement in medicine come?

The completion of the human genome project is the most major advancement medicine has made in the past ten years. It is the precursor of a lot of medical advances. In the future, I believe everybody will be able to have their genome screened at an affordable price so they will know every disease they are predisposed to. This will help preventative medicine. Also, it will allow for more specialized treatments. Farther in the future, I believe we will be able to routinely perform gene therapy procedures.

96. Is there anything in the history of medicine that fascinates you?

Edward Jenner used a medical observation (the fact that cowpox prevents smallpox) that led to the discovery of vaccinations. This discovery led to a better understanding of antibodies and the immune system.

Random and annoying

97. If you do not get into medical school, what will you do?

I would figure out what was wrong with my application, fix it, and reapply.

98. Tell me about a system that was flawed and what you did to improve it.

My university has a problem recruiting culturally diverse and international students, and when they do come, they have a high rate of transferring out. I believe this is due to lack of systems to help them integrate into the new culture. Coming from a diverse family in Miami, I definitely felt a culture shock living in North Carolina. I had a friend from Miami who was going through the same thing. She was actually ready to transfer to the University of Miami. I did some research and discovered that the university had an organization of Latin American students, but it did not have a big presence on campus. We joined the group and worked to recruit more students and increase awareness about the organization throughout the campus.

This past fall, when all the new Latin American students came to the campus, they did not have to feel they were on their own. This is not to say that all Hispanics should hang out together, but it helps diverse students assimilate into the culture by giving them a little reminder of home, making them feel welcome, offering them mentorship, and letting them know that there are people like them that have gone through the same thing or are going through the same thing. We have our own dinners and intramural sports teams; we share our experiences and often have guest speakers come to the campus to talk to the student body about issues such as immigration and affirmative action. We also do a lot of service work like tutoring at a local middle school, inviting children on campus to trick-or-treat and play games. My little sister is a sophomore at my university, and she constantly tells me how thankful she is to have the organization there for her. Knowing that I am graduating, she is taking on a bigger role in the organization too.

99. What are the negative aspects of your clinical experience?

I was shadowing a physician, and he was looking over an X-ray of a shoulder joint replacement with his fellow. He was explaining that whoever had done that procedure used a ball that was too big and that was what was restricting the patient's mobility. Either the physician could tell the patient that the previous doctor had made a big mistake, which would have thrown the other physician under the bus, angered the patient, and put himself in a difficult situation, or he could take the easy route and just tell the patient that this was just a normal consequence of the procedure. He did the latter. This greatly upset me, and I told myself that if I am ever in that position, I will do what is best for the patient, even if it is a more challenging path. Also, if I were the physician and I saw another physician doing something like that, I would confront him about it.

100. What book have you read recently that has had a profound effect on your life? What is your favorite book?

A Brief History of Time by Stephen Hawking. Although this book did not have an impact on the way I live my life, it did have an impact on the way I look at life and the universe. Hawking takes abstract physical concepts and puts them into terms so that somebody without a physics degree can understand. He explains that if you went into a time machine, you could never get to the beginning of the big bang because time itself started with the big bang. Also, you could never watch the big bang happen because space itself started with the big bang. This type of thinking is really fascinating to me.

101. Have you ever had a frustrating experience with a group member or coworker?

Yes, in my biology lab my first semester, we had a group presentation due the day after Thanksgiving break. We all went home for the break and agreed to work on our portions of the presentation individually. I had the discussion, so I needed the person who was writing the introduction to send me a draft as soon as possible so that I could build off it. I constantly called the girl, asking when she would have something to show me. It was not until the night before the presentation that she sent me a few worthless slides. I stayed up all night creating an introduction and discussion and scheduled a morning meeting to tell her what she needed to say. We aced the presentation, but it was very frustrating to see her walk away with the same grade as me.

102. If you could not pursue a career in the medical field, what would you do?

I would explore my interest in engineering because I love science and creativity. However, my brother is an engineer, and he spends most of his day in front of a computer. It would be sad to not be able to make that deep human connection.

103. Who inspires you? Who is your hero? Who is your role model?

My mom is my role model. Her father escaped Cuba on a raft. She was born and raised in Cuba and, after a lot of hard work and perseverance, became a dermatologist. She is also a great mother of five kids. Despite her amazing success, she is very humble, loving, and fun. I have not had to face such a difficult situation, but she still inspires me to reach my dreams and be a good person.

104. What would you have done differently than your role model?

My mom went into dermatology, and I will probably not choose that as a specialty. I like MOHS surgery but not cosmetic stuff.

105. What is a characteristic of your role model that you do not want to have?

My mom donates a lot to charity, but she still really enjoys expensive things. I have no interest in expensive things, and I do not want to.

106. Who, besides your parents, inspires you? Who is the greatest leader that you know?

Besides my parents, I am inspired by my best friend. As a high school football superstar, he was extremely humble, hardworking, and fun to be around. After signing a full scholarship to ___ university, he missed his entire freshman year because of a devastating shoulder injury that eventually got infected. He lost over forty pounds in a few months and was struggling just to walk to his classes. Throughout the entire struggle, he was not down on himself; he was the same funny, optimistic person. Once he was cleared to begin training again, he trained relentlessly for over a year and is now on track to rotate in with the starting defense this fall. Even as a college football star, he is still the same humble, hardworking, happy friend. He has demonstrated the importance of maintaining these characteristics throughout the highs and lows of life and has inspired me to do the same.

107. What do you see as challenges in medical school? What would be your greatest impediment to succeeding in this program?

The workload and constant stress, but my undergraduate career has trained me well.

108. Is medicine a right or a privilege?

It is a privilege because it is a service that has expenses, including time, money, energy, and risks. However, it is a privilege that should be made accessible to more people.

109. We obviously have compassion for patients with diseases like cancer, but how do you feel about treating people who cause their own diseases?

We need to bring the same compassion for all patients and make it a point not to look down on them. Physicians are in a great position to connect with people and initiate lifestyle changes that improve their health.

110. How do you cope with people who do not live up to your expectations? What do you do if a member of your group does not do his share of the work?

I would first tell the person directly that they are not doing enough. If they do not change, I would find out if there is a possibility of finding a replacement. If that is not an option, I would just have to work harder to pick up the slack.

111. If you could change one thing about your university, what would it be?

Diversity.

112. If you could change anything about your undergraduate education, what would it be?

I would increase the number of classes available. It is so difficult for underclassmen to get into the courses they want because they all fill up. I wanted to take a course on Asian history with a professor who had great ratings, but by the time I got to register, the class was full. I ended up taking a Western civilization course with an incredibly boring professor.

113. If you could have dinner with one person, dead or alive, who would it be? If you could be any character in history, who would it be, and why?

Gandhi. Using nonviolent civil disobedience, he led India to independence and inspired nonviolent freedom movements across the world, including our own civil rights movement in the United States. I would ask him what inspired him to lead a nonviolent revolution.

114. Regardless of your grade, what course would you recommend all students take?

History of Western Art. This class improved my appreciation for art. I would recommend it to all students because it allows you to see how many facets of art and human perceptions changed with civilization, while many have stayed the same for thousands of years. Regardless of profession, this allows you to be a more well-rounded person, with a better understanding of the world. Also, studying art is very enjoyable.

115. What do you think of the MCAT?

It is a good test in the sciences because it finds out how much you know and how quickly you can process new information. I do not like the verbal reasoning part because there is not enough time to finish all the passages and questions. If it takes me a little bit longer to do the reading, what correlation does that have with my ability to practice medicine? I have aced all of my English and humanities classes; if it takes me more time to complete the reading, I will put in extra time and do a good job.

116. Do you play instruments?

No. I love all kinds of music, and I took piano classes for five years; but as I got older, I focused more on sports. Sadly, the only thing I remember about piano is how to play "Mary Had a Little Lamb."

117. Have you had any philosophy classes? What was the favorite thing you learned?

I have not had any philosophy classes, but I have taken three religion classes. My favorite class was progressive religion and the black freedom struggle. We talked about the religion, philosophy, and politics involved in uplifting minority groups, while focusing on the freedom movement of African Americans over the centuries. I like the debate between Washington and DuBois.

118. Is there any well-run government health program?

The Veterans Health Administration is well-run because it effectively uses electronic medical records and evidence-based medicine to improve results, while reducing risks and costs.

119. Why don't you go into public health if you want to heal a lot of people?

Physicians have the unique ability to make personal connections that can have a deep impact on the lives of individual patients.

120. Why did you choose your present course of studies?

I chose to pursue a biology major, chemistry minor, and diverse liberal arts education. I am fascinated by both biology and chemistry and enjoy learning about each of them. I was originally going to do a double major but decided to drop my chemistry major to a minor in order to graduate early. I chose to pursue a liberal arts education because a major part of education is learning how to think and learn. By studying a diverse array of subjects, I am familiar with different modes of asking questions, thinking, and learning. I also do not like to be completely uneducated in entire subjects. Our modern society is so interconnected that it is essential to at least have a basic grasp of different fields of study.

121. What is your favorite subject in your present course of studies?

My favorite subject is chemistry. Understanding how the universe works at the molecular level is fascinating to me. I also find chemistry to be the most mentally stimulating subject because it requires memorization, understanding, critical thinking, and math.

122. Would you consider a career in your present course of studies?

Medicine is the ultimate career in biology!

123. Describe a situation where your work was criticized. What was your immediate reaction? Reflecting back now, what do you make of it now?

In college football, we watched every play of every practice from two aerial angles in slow motion with our position group. I could do almost everything right on a play and score a touchdown, and all the coach would say was, "You did this wrong." It was difficult to accept criticism on the football field because I worked so hard to perfect my craft. However, I was able to learn how to accept criticism because I knew it would make me better and improve my skills. I am extremely thankful that I learned how to accept criticism because I now know that it is essential for improving.

124. What have you done that shows initiative? What did you learn from that experience?

I wanted to conduct a research and get more clinical experience, so I took the initiative to design a research project and find physicians in the Dominican Republic that were willing to support me with my research and provide me clinical experience. I then took the initiative to apply for a scholarship to fund this project. The clinical experience in the DR has cemented my conviction about becoming a physician. The research experience was great, and I recently submitted my article to the *Journal of Parasitology* for review.

125. If you could have dinner with one living person today, who would it be?

I would have dinner with President Obama because he is the leader of the free world. I would ask him why he was unable to shut down Guantanamo Bay, why he has not addressed the malpractice issue in medicine, and if he truly believes that the quality of medicine will not go down with Obamacare. I would also talk to him about his plan to combat illegal and prescription drug abuse in the United States.

126. Think of a person who has helped you the most in your life. Describe what they did and said, and the lasting impact they have had on you.

The person who has helped me the most in my life is my mother. Her support and guidance have been at the root of every success I have had. However, what she has done more than anything else is inspire me. Her father escaped Cuba with no education, money, or English. She was born and raised in Cuba and, after an incredible amount of hard work and perseverance, has became a dermatologist and mother of five children. Despite her success, she has remained a humble, fun, and loving person. She instilled these values in me from a young age and continues to inspire me to be the best person I can.

127. Can you define any of your personal qualities that are beneficial for a good doctor and three of your qualities you should improve to be able to become a better doctor?

I am hardworking. I would improve my overcommitment. I would be better at making jokes. I would be able to speak more languages.

128. Why didn't you go into social work if you like working with people?

I love working with people, but I am passionate about making a significant difference in people's lives. The ultimate way to do that is through medicine. After shadowing many physicians, I have seen the deep impact they have on people's lives. After working in the medical missions in Santo Domingo, I have experienced what if feels like to help treat people medically and have concluded that medicine goes far beyond any other forms of service work.

Also, I love science, research, and learning; but science on its own does not provide me with that deep human connection that is so important to me. I believe medicine is the ultimate balance between science and humanitarianism. I also believe that medical research allows for a more far-reaching and long-lasting impact.

129. Tell me about your most valued mentor.

My best friend is my most valued mentor. Throughout high school, he constantly pushed me to train as hard as possible. When I was doing well, he made sure I stayed humble and kept training. In my senior year, when I was still not being recruited anywhere, he told me to keep my head up, keep working, and keep doing what I love. I was eventually recruited to a division 1 team. When I had to walk away from football, I went through an identity crisis, but he explained to me that my value and identity do not come from my ability to play football—they come from my character. He said that the same attitude that I brought to football would drive me to success in everything I put my heart into. This support is what allowed me to continue pursuing the premed track without stumbling over this major obstacle in my life.

130. A lot of physicians do not spend enough time with their patients. How would you make sure you relate with your patients?

A lot of physicians do this to make more profit. I really do not like the idea of thinking of the patient as a client. That is part of the reason I want to work in academic medicine. I want to be able to take whatever time is necessary to treat the patient. I understand the importance of this because I have been a patient in this kind of situation. After doing months of rehab to try to make it back to spring practice, the orthopedist sat me down and said that he could clear me but that I needed to understand the decision I was making. That allowed me to make the best decision. He seemed invested in my situation but allowed me to make the decision for myself. I want to be able to do the same for my patients.

131. Give an example of a leadership role you have assumed.

I was the captain of the varsity football team for my junior and senior years in high school. This was an extremely important role for me because high school football in Miami is extremely competitive. I led the team in workouts and practices. During games, I was responsible for choosing defensive plays based on what the opposing team was doing and communicating those decisions to the rest of the defense before the play. I also had to know everybody's assignment, in case anybody forgot. When people made mistakes, instead of yelling at them, I taught them what they were doing wrong and how to correct them. These skills are obviously very important for a physician because of the amount of collaboration that takes place in modern medicine.

132. What are the most important qualities in being a good doctor?

Integrity, compassion, affability, work ethic, and intelligence.

133. Tell me of an ethical dilemma and how you decided what to do.

I was shadowing a physician, and he was looking over an X-ray of a shoulder joint replacement with his fellow. He was explaining that whoever had done that procedure used a ball that was too big and that was what was restricting the patient's mobility. Either the physician could tell the patient that the previous doctor had made a big mistake, which would have thrown the other physician under the bus, angered the patient, and put himself in a difficult situation, or he could take the easy route and just tell the patient that this was just a normal consequence of the procedure. He did the latter. I felt the need to speak up and tell the patient what was really going on, but I knew it was not my place, as a college student, to challenge the surgeon. I asked my parents if I should have said something, and they agreed there was nothing I could have done. This greatly upset me, and I told myself that if I am ever in that position, I will do what is best for the patient, even if it is a more challenging path. Also, if I were a physician and I saw another physician doing something like that, I would speak up.

134. Have you done any volunteer work?

Yes. In high school I began volunteering for Habitat for Humanity, and I coached the local youth football team. In college, I continued working for Habitat, and I also tutored and gave talks at local middle schools. Two summers ago, I was a volunteer counselor at Camp Discovery, which is a camp for kids with chronic skin conditions.

I really enjoyed all of those volunteer experiences, but my most rewarding experience was this past summer in the Dominican. While working in the medical clinics, I was able to help provide care and connect with patients. This was far more rewarding than any other volunteer experience I had had before. This experience is actually what cemented my decision about practicing medicine.

135. How do you handle stress? Describe a support system you have adopted or relied upon to handle stress. Give me an example of when you solved a tough problem. What approach did you use?

I handle stress by overpreparing. This allows me to be confident, focused, and relaxed when it is time to perform.

136. What do you do with your spare time?

It has been difficult to find spare time, but I make sure that I make time for myself to stay sane. I try to spend it relaxing with friends and family. My younger sister goes to the same university, so we try to meet up for lunch and dinner as much as possible. Now that I am no longer playing football, I consider working out as part of my spare time because it is a way for me to release stress. I also love wakeboarding, spearfishing, and paintballing but have not had a lot of opportunities to go in the past few years.

137. Tell me about a time you had to convince someone to do something they did not want to do.

As a football captain, I had to constantly convince teammates to do the extra nonmandatory workouts on the weekends. I just told them that their training would make the team better, and we wanted to make a run at the state championship this year.

138. What is wrong with the application process?

I have been happy with the overall process, but if I had to change something, it would be to get rid of the verbal reasoning section of the MCAT. If a student can do well in their literature courses, then why does it matter how many passages he can read in an hour? Nobody times me when I do my reading assignments in school; if I need more time to complete my reading, I will spend more time reading. I do not believe that my ability to analyze random passages is correlated with my ability to be a good physician. This section of the test was also the most difficult to study for.

139. What could you have done better as an undergraduate student to prepare for medical school? What would you have done differently?

Taking more psychology and sociology courses would help me be more prepared for the personal side of medicine, but I am confident that I will learn the essentials of psychology and sociology in medical school.

140. What is the best advice anybody has given you?

The best advice I have ever been given is to seek advice.

141. What are some of the things that you will have to give up as a doctor?

I do not think I will have to give up anything. I will have to put in a great deal of time and energy, but that is not a sacrifice. It is a privilege because I would rather not put that time and energy on anything else.

142. Describe a project in which you worked in a team. What is your role on a team?

I can play whatever role is required of me, from leader to team player. I had been playing football since I was ten years old, which required me to learn how to work on a team. In high school, I was elected captain as a junior and a senior. This required me to make important decisions quickly and communicate them to the rest of the team. It also required me to lead the team through what I say and what I do.

While I was playing college football, we had to work together as a team in everything we did. In order to make it through training camp, we had to be there to support each other. Oftentimes, I would have to be willing to switch roles with another player in order to put the team in a better position, even if it meant that I was not the one making the play.

Being able to play different roles on a team is extremely important in modern medicine because of all the collaboration that occurs in the clinical and research worlds. Sometimes a physician is the head surgeon of a large operation, and he needs to know how to be a leader. Sometimes a physician is a resident in an emergency situation; and he has to be comfortable taking orders, communicating, and doing whatever it takes to help the team win.

143. If you could change one thing about yourself, what would it be?

Nothing. I am not perfect, but my flaws make me who I am, and I am happy with the person I am today.

144. What do you think about the new MCAT?

I like that the new MCAT is trying to adapt to the changing field of medicine by adding sections on psychology and sociology and adding questions based on passages in social sciences, humanities, ethics, and cross-cultural studies.

I believe that the cause is noble, but in practicality, it does not make sense to give multiple-choice questions in subjects that usually do not have only one right answer to the questions. Also, ensuring that a student can select the right answer on a multiple-choice ethics question does not ensure that he will act ethically. Ensuring that a student selects the right answer on a cross-cultural studies question does not ensure that the student has the ability to connect with people from different cultures.

145. What has been your greatest success?

In high school, I did not have the same work ethic in my academic as I did in college, and this caused my academic work to feel like more of a chore than something to be enjoyed. In college, I was able to transfer the work ethic and intensity that I learned from football to other aspects of my life, including academics. Being able to make this shift allowed me to excel in the classroom and enjoy the learning experience, while playing football at the highest collegiate level. I also brought that same intensity to my exploration in the field of medicine, so I would say my greatest success was being able to make that shift.

146. What has been your biggest failure?

My biggest failure was the fact that I never got to play division 1-A varsity football in a game. I trained extremely hard to get to the position to be able to play, but my injury would not let me. Although this was a difficult failure to swallow, it led to many great opportunities. It allowed me to deeply explore my interest in medicine and graduate a semester early.

147. Tell me about a mentorship role you have assumed.

My little sister is a premed at my university, so I have constantly been a mentor to her. In addition to helping her improve her study skills and make her schedule every semester, I have provided her personal support and guidance and helped her get acclimated to college.

148. How do you solve interpersonal conflicts?

I remain calm no matter what, and I communicate with the other person in a respectful way in a low voice. I try to understand where they are coming from so that we can reach a solution together.

149. Tell me about your women and gender studies class.

It was a one-credit pass/fail class with no regular lectures. We just had to go to seven different talks or performances dealing with women and gender studies and write a two-page reflection on each one. I would not say that I learned a lot, but the course opened my eyes to different perspectives.

150. How do you study/prepare for exams?

After every lecture, I type my notes, using PowerPoint, the textbook, and the Internet as guides. If there is anything I do not fully understand, I make sure to meet with my professor about it as soon as possible. When the test is nearing, I make a copy of all my notes, delete the things I already know, and focus on learning the things that I do not know. I then go through all the practice problems and take notes on any questions that I got wrong or struggled with.

151. Do you engage in self-directed learning?

Yes. Although most of my classes in college have been lecture based, they often stimulate self-directed learning. The basic information is usually presented in lecture and PowerPoint, but in order to fully understand the material, I have to go back and teach it to myself on my whiteboard. This allows me to think critically about what I am learning so that I can apply it to different or changing situations.

I also take the initiative to explore subjects that interest me. I wanted to conduct research and get more clinical experience, so I designed a research project and found physicians in the Dominican Republic that were willing to support me with my research and provide me clinical experience. I then applied for a scholarship to fund this project. The clinical experience in the DR has cemented my conviction about becoming a physician. The research experience was great, and I recently submitted my article to the *Journal of Parasitology* for review.

152. If you had three magical wishes, what would they be?

    a. Everybody in the world to be cured of all diseases. There would still be a need for doctors because people still break bones and give births. This would cause a problem with limited food resources.

    b. End world hunger. With so many healthy, well-fed people, I would want to make sure they all get along.

    c. World peace.

153. How would you attract physicians to rural areas?

Helping physicians pay for student loans would help. Requiring people to work in a rural area for a year could be a potential solution. In the Dominican, they require their physicians to do a year of rural clinics before practicing.

154. Describe a positive and negative experience in your undergraduate training.

History class was the worst experience. The lecturer could not stay on topic and had no structure, and I could not see its relevance to my life. However, after taking the History of Western Art, I gained an appreciation for what I learned in my history class. My first biology class was amazing. I loved the material, and the professor taught me good study habits. I also learned that if I put in enough work, I could do well in any class.

155. What is the best thing that has ever happened to you?

Aside from having an amazing family, the best thing that has happened to me was going to my university. It has been such an amazing experience.

156. What negative experiences from your different jobs made it clear to you that you wanted to pursue medicine?

I did not have any really negative experiences. Although I have enjoyed the research I have done in biology and chemistry labs, science on its own does not provide me with that deep human connection that is so important to me. I believe medicine is the ultimate balance between science and humanitarianism, and as a physician, I still plan to do research that will have a far-reaching, long-lasting impact.

157. Are you introverted or extroverted? How will this impact how you communicate with patients and coworkers?

I am an introvert with a significant amount of leadership and group-work experiences. I have the compassion and understanding to carefully consider what people tell me before responding. I also have the confidence and voice necessary to express myself clearly, concisely, and respectfully, whether it be in front of a large group or a single person. These characteristics will allow me to learn how to build intimate relationships with patients and colleagues, while being a team player and leader, when necessary.

158. Tell me a joke.

A lion and a cheetah enter a race. The cheetah wins. The lion says, "You cheetah." The cheetah says, "Nah, you lion."

159. Teach me something.

I can teach you how to say "I am going to accept you into my medical school" in Spanish.

160. Describe a time when you felt you were "at your best."

I have felt "at my best" ever since beginning college. I began enjoying my learning and extracurricular experiences, which allowed me to put in the time and energy necessary to excel. This made it clear to me that when I am passionate about what I am doing, I will succeed. This will benefit me as a physician because I am passionate about practicing medicine, teaching, and conducting research.

161. Describe another experience that influenced you in a significant way.

In one of the clinics in the Dominican Republic, I had to explain to a seven-year-old boy that the physicians were going to have to draw blood from his arm. He started throwing a fit, but I told him we were going to have to do it anyway, so he might as well make it easy. I also told him that it does not hurt very much and that he could squeeze my hand as they were drawing his blood. When it was time to draw blood, he told the physician that he wanted me to do it. I told him I was not trained to do that, but he could still squeeze my hand. We drew blood, and afterward he admitted that it did not hurt very much. Being able to connect with him in a way that earned his trust was an amazing feeling.

162. What do you think you will like most about medicine?

I will love having the privilege to treat people and save lives.

163. What would you do on a perfect day?

I would go spearfishing with my family in Miami all day. We would then have a big fish cookout at our house with my friends and family, including my extended family. Later at night, we would have a bonfire in the backyard and sit around telling stories and jokes.

164. Provide an example of a time you needed help. Tell me about a time you were in need.

While scuba diving, I ran out of air and had to quickly and calmly swim to my dad to use his extra regulator.

165. Tell me about a time that made you angry. How do you deal with anger?

I almost never get angry. However, once, I was with a group of people at a social gathering, and everybody wanted to leave except one person. We finally convinced the person to leave. On the cab ride back, the person was yelling profanities at everybody in the car because this person wanted to stay. This made me angry because the person was being so disrespectful and self-centered. I normally try to calm myself down and emotionally separate myself from the situation.

166. What else do you want to accomplish in life besides attending medical school?

I want to be the best physician I can be. I want to make a significant finding in my research that advances the field of medicine. I want to volunteer my time in international medical missions. I want to be able to teach medicine. I also want to have a family, and I want to be able to support my kids in doing whatever it is they are passionate about because I would not have been able to accomplish what I have without the support of my family.

167. Why study medicine when you have so many talents?

Thank you for the compliment. I would say that, currently, my most meaningful talents are my abilities to learn, think critically, and connect with people. The best use of these talents is in medicine because they are required of a good doctor, and practicing medicine is the greatest privilege somebody can have.

168. Which of your accomplishments on your AMCAS application do you consider your biggest success? Your biggest failure?

My biggest success is that I was able to maintain a GPA above 3.9 while playing division 1-A varsity football. My biggest failure is that I did not do more volunteer work. However, the volunteer work I did had a huge impact on me.

169. Tell me about this award/experience on your AMCAS application.

170. Can you show that you have compassion?

Yes. It is difficult to show compassion through what you say, but I can tell you about what I have done in medical clinics.

171. Can you show that you have intellectual curiosity?

Yes. I have a diverse liberal arts education and have worked on multiple research projects, including one that I though of, designed, received funding for, carried out, and wrote all on my own.

172. Can you show that you have adaptability?

Yes. I quickly adapted to the new culture of North Carolina. Also, I went to a liberal arts school, so I had to take a wide variety of classes. It takes a great deal of adaptability for a biology major to write essays on Renaissance paintings.

173. Do you have a favorite quote?

"Impossible is just a big word thrown around by small men who find it easier to live the world they have been given, rather than to explore the power they have to change it. Impossible is not a fact. It is an opinion. Impossible is not a declaration. It is a dare. Impossible is potential. Impossible is temporary. Impossible is nothing."

174. How can you tell if someone is truly compassionate?

It is difficult to do so by just listening to what they say. However, even when only considering what they tell you about their experiences, someone who is truly compassionate tends to look you in the eye and have a distinct tone of sincerity in their voice.

175. When was the last time you told a lie?

The last time I told a lie was when I bought my plane tickets here. I lied that I read and agreed to the terms and conditions on the website.

176. If you could not go into anything related to science, what would you do?

I would be some kind of social worker or teacher, where I get a lot of interaction with students. However, it would be sad to not make that deep human connection and help people in such a deep way. It would also be unfortunate to not be able to satisfy my desire for scientific understanding and research.

177. Why become a physician instead of a PA or something?

I really want to make as great of an impact as I can on patients and in the field of medicine. I do not want to be restricted by the degree I hold.

178. What is the most creative thing you have ever done?

Spearguns are illegal in the Bahamas, so when spearfishing there, everybody has to use a Hawaiian sling, which is like a slingshot with a spear. The only problem is that the spear is not attached to the sling, so unless you kill the fish when you shoot it, the fish can just swim away. I put a reel on a Hawaiian sling.

179. What is informed consent?

In order to give informed consent, a patient must have competence, adequate information, and no coercion. The patient must be aware of the nature, cost, risk, and benefits of the proposed medical action and give consent to the physician.

189. What is the funniest thing that has ever happened to you?

I was on a road trip with my family, and we stopped for food. My little brother was barely chewing, and I kept telling him to take his time. About an hour later in the trip, he made us pull over. He threw up huge chunks of hot dogs and a big ball of gum. I felt bad for him but could not stop laughing.

190. What is the most fun thing you have ever done?

I frequently go spearfishing with my friends and family. I love it because it is a great bonding experience, and it feels like entering another world.

191. What is the most rewarding/satisfying thing you have ever done? Describe the moment when you felt the happiest.

Working in the medical clinics in the Dominican was amazing because I got to help provide medical care to people in need.

192. What do you think about when you are alone?

I am an introvert, so I think about a lot of things on my own. At the end of every day, I like to spend some time alone, reflect on my day, and think about my plans for the future. I like to constantly remind myself how lucky I am; it helps me put everything into perspective.

193. Why are some doctors unhappy practicing medicine?

Many physicians work so hard and are so constantly stressed that they do not get to enjoy their work or their lives outside of work. Some have high-risk specialties in places where malpractice cases are common. Also, patients may not follow orders, which could get frustrating.

194. Describe what you believe is the appropriate relationship between a physician and a nurse?

The physician is responsible for making the decisions and for communicating that to the nurse and the patient. The nurse is responsible for carrying out the physician's orders. Like in any team, success relies on mutual respect and communication. I believe that oftentimes physicians feel they are superior to nurses and do not respect their work. This fact, the lack of communication, and the stress of the hospital, causes the relationship to deteriorate. This is detrimental to patient care. I believe we need to put more emphasis on educating doctors and nurses to respect each other and communicate effectively.

195. What is the most important development in the world over the past twenty-five years?

Making the Internet available to the general public revolutionized the way we access information and communicate with each other.

196. What vegetable would you be?

I would be a carrot because my core values are deep and strongly rooted.

197. What fruit would you be?

I would be a coconut because I can withstand a lot without falling apart.

198. What tree would you be?

I would be a coconut tree because can adapt to soils with a wide range of salinities.

199. What is the Hippocratic oath?

It is an oath taken by physicians to practice medicine ethically. This means to treat the ill to the best of their ability, to do no harm, to respect patient privacy and autonomy, and to educate the next generation.

200. Are you willing to work in a rural area?

I am open to anything. However, I see myself working in an urban area and getting involved in medical clinics in underserved areas, regardless of their settings.

201. Do you fear failure?

No. I embrace my failures because I know they are just part of the path to success. The minute I start to fear failure is the minute I extinguish my chances of finding success.

202. How do you think you did in this interview?

I think I did well. I gave you very honest, sincere answers to all of your questions. I believe I made it clear that I have studied the field of medicine and cemented my convictions about practicing medicine. Also,

I believe I have shown that I have the integrity, honesty, and physical and mental strength necessary to become a physician.

203. Who is the surgeon general?

Regina Benjamin. She is the head of the Public Health Service Commissioned Corps. She also has to educate the American public about health.

204. What is family practice, and what is the biggest problem they face?

Family practice focuses on the patient in the context of the family and the community. It emphasizes disease prevention and health promotion. Just like other physicians, the biggest problem they face is that they have to tell patients that there is nothing we can do to help them.

205. What makes you sad?

Seeing people suffer makes me very sad, especially when there are people who could help them but choose not to. I was sad in Santo Domingo when I saw so many people suffering from poverty, while a few wealthy people down the street did not seem to care.

206. What articles have you read recently that make you want to become a physician?

The one that comes to mind is more of an essay. It was a medical resident's account of her experience with her first patient who died. It is very sad, but she speaks about the connection she was able to make with the patient and the family, the impact she was able to make on their lives, and the care she was able to provide. She expresses a great deal of satisfaction, purpose, and passion in the essay.

207. If you love research so much, why are you not pursuing an MD-PhD degree?

I have given that some serious thought. However, I want to focus on patient care, and I have also learned that with the amount of collaboration that goes on in modern research, it is not essential to have a PhD degree to do meaningful research as a physician. The head of my university's medical research department does not have a PhD.

208. What makes you a fun person?

I am down-to-earth, nonjudgmental, and relaxed. I like to joke and tell stories. I am into extreme sports like spearfishing, paintballing, and wakeboarding. I can also relate to a lot of different people because of my multicultural upbringing.

209. Is there anything nonmedical that scares you?

I am afraid of death. However, the fact that it will inevitably come makes me really emphasize living my life to the fullest. To me, that means making a significant impact on the world, enjoying my time here, and taking risks.

210. Tell me about a risk you have taken.

Everything in life is a risk; the only thing that changes is the odds. A significant risk I took was going to North Carolina for college. I could have stayed at home and gone to an easier school, where I was used to the city, and had an easier time in the classroom and in the football field. I chose to go to a new state, with a different culture and much more serious academics and football. It was a huge risk, and it was the greatest thing that ever happened to me.

211. What is the wackiest/craziest thing you ever did?

I grew dreadlocks for a while in the summer after my freshman year in college. I had always wanted to do it because I have thick curly hair. It was funny and entertaining to see people's reactions, but I eventually got it out of my system.

212. Have you taught yourself anything?

I taught myself how to write in Spanish. During my first semester in college, I was placed in the highest-level Spanish class because I grew up speaking Spanish. However, I never really had to read or write in Spanish before, and in this class we read poetry and plays and wrote essays about them. I had to sit down for hours to learn the rules for placing accents and spelling.

213. If you could be any cell in the human body, which cell would it be?

I would be a brain cell because of the amount of information they take in and put out and the amount of connections that they make with other cells.

214. If you could build a human body, what would you include and exclude?

I would leave out some greed, jealousy, revenge, and close-mindedness. I would add more creativeness, passion, and compassion.

School-specific

Admissions committees want to know that if they accept you, you will go to their school. They also want to know that you're the type of person who does their research before going into a situation. Before going for an interview at any school, I had to convince myself that I had always dreamed of going to that school and living in that city. I bought the Medical School Admission Requirement (MSAR) online book and read what it had to say about every school. Using that information, I would talk the school up in my head.

215. Why do you want to go to this school? Why do you think you would be a good fit for this program? Why did you decide to apply to this school?

The missions of this school closely resonate with my values and goals. In addition to patient care, I plan to do a significant amount of research, teaching, and service as a medical student and as a physician.

There is an incredible amount of research opportunities. This is very important to me because I plan to continue conducting research as a medical student and as a physician.

I love the fact that there is a holistic, patient-centered approach to learning with programs like the family-centered experience. I like that students begin practicing clinical skills in the first year. Perfecting those skills is essential to becoming a good physician, and I am excited to begin practicing them.

I also like that the first two years is P/F because this creates a family environment and allows for teamwork and collaboration.

The other important factor is service. I have loved my community service experiences, especially working in medical clinics in the Dominican. I plan to continue working in medically underserved communities nationally and internationally as a med student and as a physician. This school makes it possible for students to have global health experiences. Fifty-seven percent of graduates have a global health experience, in addition to the local service opportunities.

This school is the perfect match for me in every way. Thank you very much.

216. What research projects at this school interest you the most?

The department of human genetics has several fascinating labs. Dr. _____'s lab does great research on the genetics of diseases of the peripheral nervous system. I do not know specifically what lab I will work in, but this is a huge institution with many opportunities for collaboration, so I am sure I will find my niche. I know the ___ Institute for Clinical and Health Research does a great job of helping students find a research program that they are passionate about.

217. You say in your secondary application that you did ___ in this city. Can you tell me a little bit more about that experience?

218. What is the aspect of this med school that you like the least?

a. The location. The only family I have in the United States is in South Florida, so living in __ will make it somewhat difficult to visit them. This is nothing new to me. When I was living in North Carolina and playing football, I would go several months without seeing any of my family. Also, working in Boston, I have not been able to visit any family. I always put my education first, and I think _____ would be a perfect match.

b. I know that in the broad sense of the term, the student body here is very diverse, but in terms of ethnic diversity, it is somewhat limited. There were only __ Hispanic students in last year's class. This is nothing new to me, but I would have liked to see a more diverse student body.

219. What is your number 1 school?

Harvard. The amount of research opportunities and clinical experiences there is unbelievable.

220. Where else are you applying?

All the schools in my state and other major research institutes on this side of the country. The reason I applied to so many schools is that my primary goal is just to get into medical school.

221. If you are accepted here, will you come?

If you accept me right now, I will cancel my other travel plans and come right now. If in March I am accepted here and in another top research school, it will be a difficult decision.

222. Where do you plan to practice?

Ideally, I will practice in Florida, but I am open to practicing anywhere.

223. Do you have any questions for me? (Physician)

I am really interested in working in the student-run clinics. Do you know how much of a role first—and second-year students get to play in those? What type of formal mentorship program is there for students who are trying to decide what residency program to go into?
(For a student, you can say the same things as above, or you can say this.) How do you like living here? Why did you choose to come here? Is there anything about this school you would change?

224. So you were raided in Miami, and all of your family in the United States is in South Florida? Are you really going to go to school in ___?

Well actually, I was born in St. Louis, moved to Miami when I was four, moved to North Carolina when I was seventeen, and am currently working in Boston. I am the type of person that can be happy anywhere you put me. I am not going to let geography determine the quality of my education. Miami is a great place to live but a difficult place to study. I actually prefer to be somewhere where I do not have so many friends and family so I can focus on my work. Besides, ___ is a great city that has a lot of ___ and ___.

SAL EKTMI

CHAPTER 2

Interview Insight

I WILL TELL you a little bit more about my interview experience to help you know what to expect. I sent twenty primary applications in June. One school rejected me without sending me a secondary application. I withdrew my applications from five schools before hearing if they wanted to interview me. Six schools rejected me without an interview. In September, I completed three interviews. In October, I completed two interviews and received three acceptances. In November, I completed one interview and received a $15,000/year scholarship offer from one of the schools that had already accepted me. In December, I completed one interview and received one waiting list notification. In January, I received one acceptance. In February, I completed one interview and received one acceptance. In March, I received two waiting list notifications and a $10,000/year scholarship offer from one of the schools that had already accepted me. In May, I received acceptances from all three schools that had waitlisted me.

Do practice interviews with as many people as possible and as many times as possible. I asked everybody I could think of to interview me. The list includes my parents; my siblings; my aunt, who is a lawyer; my uncle, who is a lawyer; my girlfriend's dad, who is a lawyer; my girlfriend's mom, who is a judge; my girlfriend's mom's coworkers, who were all judges; my parents' friends and partners, who are physicians, salespeople, medical school admissions officers, and medical students; and my school's career counselors. Most of these people interviewed me multiple times. We would sit down and do the interviews as if they were real. I would wear my full suit and have them invite me to a room, sit me down, and everything. Whether they were asking me their own questions or questions from my compiled list, we would go straight through to the end of the interview, taking notes along the way. At the end, we would break, and they would give me tons of valuable feedback. I would write it all down and incorporate it all into my interview document later that day. This helped me come up with more questions, improve my answers, improve my delivery, and most of all, improve my confidence for the real interviews.

Be ready to run the entire interview. In one of my interviews, a man could not access my file or his list of questions, so I had to decide what topics I wanted to talk about. I basically interviewed myself in front of him. This gave me more liberty but put me in a situation I was not used to being in.

Be ready to answer any questions about anything on your primary or secondary applications.

I was still in college for most of my interviews and had to miss a lot of classes. I had to tell my professors how important these interviews were so that they would cut me some slack. I also kept them updated as I heard back good news from schools. I thanked them, reminding them that this was only possible because they were kind enough to let me miss classes. By the end of the semester, most of my professors were impressed and proud that I had already had many acceptances. They felt that they were part of the process and wanted me to succeed. I think this helped me a lot when it was time for final grades, especially in the more subjective courses.

Before the interview at each school, in addition to being ready to answer specific questions about that school, you should learn what the interview format is. Most schools have about two open-folder one-on-one interviews with physicians, lasting about thirty minutes. However, some schools have closed-folder interviews, some have multiple mini-interviews, some have panel interviews, some have student interviewers. Just know what to expect.

Try to stay with a student host. It is very convenient to have somebody show you where you have to go in the morning. It saves a lot of money; it gives you a perspective on what it is like to be a student there. Before going to sleep the night before the interview, set your alarm, make sure your phone is on "do not disturb mode," make sure that you have everything you need for the morning within twenty feet from where you are sleeping.

The morning of the interview, plan to get to the admissions office thirty to sixty minutes early. This will give you time to navigate through the huge medical complexes and leave room for unexpected circumstances. In one of my interviews, the taxi driver showed up fifty minutes late, but because I had told him to come an hour earlier than necessary, I still made it there on time. There is nothing wrong with getting there early. You will get to meet the other applicants and usually eat free food.

I recommend bringing mints and 5-hour Energy. Some of your interviews will be right after breakfast or lunch, so you want to make sure your breath is still good. Interviews can be exhausting, especially when you have multiple interviews in a row. I took a 5-hour Energy thirty minutes before the first interview. You want to show that you are excited, passionate, and compassionate. Try to smile as much as possible. Take your time telling the emotional and influential parts of your stories; it helps you show how much of an impact these events had on your life. It is not that these events were not seriously influential in my life, but by my eighth school, it took some conscious effort to get excited and relive the emotions behind my experiences.

Be very respectful and courteous to everybody you see on your interview day. I have been told by admissions officers that they ask everybody from secretaries to medical students if anybody showed any hints of arrogance or attitude.

Some of your interviews will be shortly after a tour. This can create problems if you need to go to the bathroom or take extra time finding your interviewer's office. I usually told the tour guide I needed to leave a little early. This gave me time to find the office, go to the bathroom, and get mentally prepared for the interview.

During your interview, you want to be relaxed but not too relaxed, confident but not overconfident, excited and passionate but not overwhelmingly emotional (you do not want to start crying). Speak with a loud, clear voice at a slow pace. Pay attention to cues as to when the interviewer wants you to keep going or stop talking. Look them in the eye as much as possible. Do not forget to thank your interviewer at the end. Realize these are busy people who are volunteering their time to get to know who you are.

If you are interviewed by a student, treat them as you would a professor, not a peer. They have the same vote as anybody else on the interview team, and they expect to be treated with the same respect.

Handwritten thank-you letters make greater impressions than e-mailed letters. On the interview day, I would bring in my bag a default thank-you letter typed on my computer and the appropriate number of envelopes with paper inside. Every school will be able to hold your bag for you in the office during your day. The envelopes were already addressed to the medical school admissions office. At the end of the interview day, I would find a quiet place where I could personalize my default letters on my computer to address my specific interviews. It helps to talk about what you talked about in your interviews so that the interviewer remembers you more specifically. Once I had the appropriate number of individualized interview documents, I would transcribe them each to the papers in my prepackaged envelopes. I then addressed each envelope to the appropriate interviewer, sealed it, and walked it back to the admissions office. This avoids any problems that could happen during shipping. It is also impressive for an interviewer to have a letter waiting for him on his desk the morning after he interviewed you. Also, it helps to write the letters immediately before you forget what you talked about in each interview. Below is a sample default letter. It should be edited for each school and for each interview.

Dear Dr. ___,

It was a pleasure to meet you this afternoon during my admissions interview for___ School of Medicine. I enjoyed learning more about the school, touring its state-of-the-art facilities, and meeting so many incredible students and faculty members. I was particularly impressed by the amount of opportunities __ provides students to get involved with research and clinical experiences. I was also impressed by the way __ integrates classroom learning with opportunities to practice clinical skills and work in medically underserved communities. I am excited about the fact that the curriculum is flexible, and there is a focus on small group study because that is the type of learning environment that allows me to excel at _____ University.

I enjoyed talking with you about the cultural diversity of ___ and how it has changed since I lived here. I am excited about the opportunity to return to ___ and play an active role in the clinics that have many Spanish-speaking patients. I also plan to get involved in interest groups that focus on cultural diversity at ___ so that I can have an experience similar to the one I had with the Organization of Latin American Students at ___ University.

SAL EKTMI

As I mentioned, I am confident that my background as a biology major has prepared me to succeed in ___'s challenging curriculum. I also believe my experience playing football developed my ability to work hard, work in teams, perform under pressure, and learn from criticism, all of which are important for a physician.

After talking with you and meeting other faculty members and students, I am more convinced than ever that ___ would be a perfect match with my experiences, interests, values, and goals. If you have any additional questions, please do not hesitate to contact me. I look forward to hearing from the admissions committee. Thank you again for taking the time to interview me.

Best Regards,
Sal Ektmi
_____@gmail.com

*   *   *

After writing your thank-you letters, you should open a new document called "thoughts on ___ medical school." You should write down everything you like and do not like about the school and the city. This will be very helpful when comparing schools because, after months of interviews, they will all start to blur together. The document does not need any organization. Just write everything you are thinking and feeling. Here is an example.

I absolutely loved ___. The people here are so nice. The town is great. It is not that hard to get to because __ is a major airport. This is a place that I can see myself calling a second home. It had really great vibes, and everybody whom I ask about ___ says they love it. There is a real family feel to the medical school and the entire university in general. I like that all the schools are on the same campus, and there is a lot to do. I love that 70 percent of the medical students live in the same building, which is walking distance from the campus. I love that there is time to chill if you want, but plenty of things to get involved in if you want. I love that campus feel. I love that they have top-ranked football and basketball teams. I love that __ is a very safe place. I love that it is a part of a big university that is so focused on providing the best care and conducting the best research. Although it is a huge medical center, there is a lot of collaboration. Classes are pass/fail, and you choose when you want to take your quizzes. The professors are very open to mentoring students. There are so many research opportunities here; it will not be hard to find a project that I love. There are plenty of volunteer opportunities. Fifty-seven percent of graduates do a global health experience. There is a patient-centered approach to learning. The simulator room was amazing, and they said people who are interested in surgery can gain twenty-four-hour card access to the room. You can practice doing laparoscopic procedures all day. They give us extra time to choose our specialty, and once you choose it, you can do specific electives that will train you to be better prepared when you go to residency. I love that there are people here from all across the country. The cost of living is low. The students all say they are not stressed and are very happy. I think I would love to go to school here. What I do not like is that it is far from all my friends and family, and the weather is so cold. It is probably my third choice, below __, but above __. It would likely be number 1 on my list if it were ranked higher or had a more prestigious name.

After you have finished all of your interviews, determine which school is your first choice. Write a letter to that school, stating that if they accept you, you will enroll immediately and withdraw your applications from all other schools.

If you are accepted by many schools, be hesitant to reject offers. Some schools have scholarship money that they use to try to draw in their favorite applicants. If they know that you are still holding a couple of acceptances, they might be more likely to offer you some money. That being said, if you are accepted to two schools and one is much better than the other, go ahead and withdraw your application to the lower school because it opens up a spot for somebody else. Money is important, but you do not want to sacrifice the quality of your education.

CHAPTER 3

Premed Insight

AT MY UNIVERSITY, about 80 percent of incoming freshmen are premed, and about 10 percent of graduating seniors are realistically still premed. The reason for these intimidating numbers is not that most people are physically unable to handle the premed process. It is that most people are not motivated enough.

Before beginning this process, ask yourself the following questions: "Why do I want to do this?" "I am willing to regularly sacrifice my social life, free time, and other activities to spend endless hours studying?" "Am I willing to undergo constant stress?" Do not begin the premed process if your motivation is money or prestige; if you spend the same time and energy preparing for any other professional career, you will find more money and prestige and a less stressful lifestyle. If you are not willing to put in constant effort and undergo serious stress, save yourself the time. If you are willing to do all these things for the right reasons, then get excited because it will all be worth it.

As a premed student, you have one asset: time. How you invest it will determine your success.

If you are still in high school, I recommend getting as much AP credit as possible, preferably science credits. When I was in high school, I did not appreciate the value of these credits. I only got AP credit for one class. My little sister got credit for three classes, and it made her process much easier.

Although taking off a year before enrolling in medical school is common, I will write the rest of this chapter with the assumption that you plan on going straight into medical school. I recommend doing summer school every year, starting the summer after high school. Summer courses are easier because you are usually just taking one class and the professors are more relaxed. I recommend taking your most difficult lectures and labs in the summer. If you can afford to do two summer sessions in a year, do it. It sounds depressing, but it is worth it. Taking summer courses also allows you to take a lighter load during the semesters. Your GPA is the single most important variable in your application. It is extremely difficult to get good grades when taking fifteen credits per semester in premed courses. I usually took about thirteen credits every semester, giving me time to excel in every course.

When planning your schedule, try to take your "MCAT-related courses" as early as possible. These include two semesters of general chemistry, two semesters of organic chemistry, two semesters of physics (one semester of calculus is a prerequisite for physics), one semester of physiology, and one semester of cellular biology. Other courses that will be helpful but are not necessary include genetics, molecular biology, biochemistry, virology, immunology, endocrinology, anatomy, evolution, ecology, and microbiology. Early planning is important because you want to take your MCAT by May of your junior year. This means you want to have your MCAT-related courses completed by the end of your fall semester junior year (your fifth semester). You can handle more later in your undergraduate career than you can freshman year; plan accordingly. Try to write out your entire schedule for semester 1-5. Obviously, some factors are unpredictable, but it is good to have a general sense of what you want to do. I recommend taking a maximum of two science lab and lecture courses each semester and a maximum of fourteen total credits. For summer courses, if you take just one science lecture and lab course, you will have plenty of free time on your hands, which is a good idea for your first summer. After your first summer, you will be able to add a little bit more to a single summer session. I would add a liberal arts course, a science course without the lab, a research course, a volunteer service, or an extracurricular activity. Taking two science lecture and lab courses in one summer session is too much.

You can major in whatever you want as a premed student; you just need to take the required premed courses. This differs for different medical schools; however, most schools require the MCAT-related courses, two semesters of literature, and a second semester of calculus. Some schools require biochemistry; most do not require biochemistry, but some do. Some schools also require statistics. I would recommend putting your intended major on the back burner until you have completed all the MCAT-related courses and your school's divisional requirements.

Most premeds do a biology major because it closely matches the premed requirements and is not as challenging as the chemistry major. The chemistry major actually matches the premed requirements more closely, but majoring in chemistry requires some intense lectures and labs, like physical chemistry. For most schools, just taking the MCAT-related courses and biochemistry (no lab required) gets you a chemistry minor, so almost everybody graduates with a chemistry minor. Also, biochemistry courses can count toward your biology credits and your chemistry credits, as long as you do not declare a biology and chemistry double major. The major and minors that you select do not have a big impact on your education. Choose something manageable that interests you.

Completing as many of your premed courses early puts you in a great position as an upperclassman. In the spring of my junior year, I realized that I could graduate a semester early if I took a course overload the next fall. This was one of the best decisions of my life. It gave me time to do whatever I wanted for eight months before starting medical school. I worked in a research lab for part of the time and just relaxed for part of the time. It was very important for me to feel rested before beginning medical school because I knew that once I started, I would not have so much freedom in a long time.

The major difference between high school and college is that, in college, a much higher percentage of your day is unscheduled. You have the freedom to do what you want with that time. Do not fall into the trap of only doing work when you have something due in the near future. You should ask, "Is there any work I can do now to help me get ahead?" and not, "Is there any work I have to do now to not fall behind?" Many classes have assignments that can be completed at any time but are not due until the end of the semester. I would spend the first few weeks of the semester completing those assignments to avoid getting overwhelmed during finals week. It's good to have some down time every now and then to relax or socialize, but if you are constantly finishing everything you can do, it is probably time to add some extracurricular activities.

Some people will tell you that you need to give up your nonmedical extracurricular activities, but I could not disagree more. My experience playing football gave me a lot to talk about in my essays and interviews. It also demonstrates a lot of character and time management skills. The truth is I had essentially no down time in college, weekends included. That was exactly what I needed to succeed. You have to be willing to spend entire weekends (Friday afternoon to Sunday night) studying.

I found that the more down time people have, the less productive they are. I knew that I had to spend every waking moment being productive, so I never slacked off. It was very intense, but football was something I was passionate about, so I was more than willing to sacrifice my down time to play. You want to have something that separates you from other applicants, and for me, it was football. Hundreds of applicants have a GPA above 3.9, but very few did it while playing varsity division 1 sports. Even after I stopped playing, I felt the need to find something else to keep me busy, so I did more volunteering and research, which was also very important to my application. You have to show that you are not just some bookworm; you are a person with experiences and passions.

When choosing extracurricular activities, you should not pick just anything to add to your resume. The medical school primary application gives you space to write about fifteen extracurricular activities and awards. For each activity, you need to say what you did, what it meant to you, and how it influenced your decision to want to go into medicine. You also have to say which months you spend doing each activity, provide the number of hours you spent in each activity per week, and give the contact information of somebody that can verify that you did this activity. It is important to shoot for quality experiences that you spent a lot of time in, not just random things that you did for a few hours every now and then. Any volunteer experience is valuable, but medically related volunteer experiences are golden. If none of your volunteer experiences were medically related, you are open to being stumped by this question: "If you love helping people so much, why not go into social work?" It is so powerful to be able to say that you experienced what it felt like to help provide medical care for people in need. If you cannot find any local hands-on opportunities, find an international medical mission. Shadowing physicians in different specialties is also good. I recommend keeping a journal for your extracurricular activities. You need to leave these experiences with influential stories; just saying you went on a mission trip is not valuable if you cannot provide any specific stories on how it impacted you. The same is true for every activity you participate in.

You will have to tie these experiences together for your personal statement. Before you begin writing this, you should just ask yourself, "Why do I want to go into medicine?" Write the most honest answer you possibly can, pretending that nobody is ever going to read it. Then try to add your experiences into the answer. You need to have a first draft of your personal statement done early so that you can edit it many times. I had everybody that I trusted help me edit my personal statement. I then had an English professor sit down with me once a week for about three months to perfect it. There are plenty of example essays, but here is mine:

Last summer, while volunteering at Camp Discovery, a camp for children with chronic skin conditions, I had the privilege of meeting ___, an eight-year-old boy who had eczema and autism. When we first met, he basically ignored me and barely spoke to anybody; his disability made it difficult for him to make friends. I made a constant effort to get to know him and eventually discovered that he had a passion for drawing pictures of zombies. Later, when it was time for the talent show, my connection with him allowed me to help him overcome his fear of being onstage. Just before the start of the show, he learned the moves and danced fantastically onstage in front of everybody. On the last day, he was singing, dancing, drawing countless zombie pictures, and explaining each one to his new friends and me in detail. Being able to connect with ___ in a way that helped him overcome his fears and grow as a person brought me a great deal of satisfaction, but more importantly, it allowed me to imagine how much more satisfying it would have been to be able to treat his eczema or autism as a physician. Although this experience did not involve any clinical work, it strengthened my desire to make a difference in the lives of others and treat people when they are sick.

Volunteering at Camp Discovery was an amazing experience, but it felt strange knowing that this was the first summer in ten years that I had not spent in football training camp. Since age ten, I aspired to play college football. By the end of my high school career, the ___ football team helped me get accepted into the university. I was determined to prove to everybody and myself that I could play at the highest level. Once at __, I made a commitment to myself to put forth the same effort in the classroom as on the football field. Two weeks before the first game of my sophomore season, I was rotating in with the starting offense and was ready to play through a nagging back injury. While getting into my stance in the middle of a hitting drill, I suddenly could not move my back at all. After getting an MRI and a CT scan, I found out I had been practicing with a stress fracture and multiple herniated discs. It seems like an obvious decision now, but walking away from the game I had dedicated so much time and energy to was one of the most challenging experiences of my life. Football developed my ability to dedicate myself to something I have a passion for, to learn from criticism, to work in a team, to perform under pressure, and to persevere. My football career did not go as planned, but it provided me the opportunity to attend a great university and to develop into a person with the characteristics necessary to excel in the medical field.

The fact that I was no longer playing college football allowed me to channel more energy into exploring ways in which I could make a significant difference in people's lives. I realized that in order to be truly satisfied, I would have to pursue a career that requires a deep compassion for others. This led me to explore my interest in medicine by shadowing an orthopedic surgeon in Miami. He treated a wide range of patients, but the one who stood out to me the most was a sprinter from a local high school. He was one of the top-ranked sprinters in the nation and was attempting to train while his knee was still seriously injured. After analyzing his MRI, the physician explained that if he kept racing, he would have knee problems for the rest of his life. In a subsequent conversation, the physician seemed more like a father than anything else. He appeared to have entered into another world, completely isolated from the hectic environment of the hospital. This was more than just another diagnosis on a busy day. At this moment, his only concern was connecting with this patient as a person in order to support him through this challenging time. What I realized then was the power physicians have to make a difference in people's lives, and the unique human responsibility they have while treating and supporting people in their most vulnerable state. I know that this is what I want to do in life; it would be a privilege and an honor to cure and connect with people on a daily basis and contribute to the field of medicine.

Over the following months, I explored my commitment by shadowing many physicians and discovered that I am fascinated by the art of medicine and by the amount of trust patients have for physicians. This trust can only be earned through selfless devotion to the well-being of others, and this is something I aspire to share with society. I am eager to dedicate my time, energy, and passion to taking care of people when they are sick because that is the ultimate way of making a difference in the lives of others.

My procedure for getting good letters of recommendation went hand in hand with my procedure for getting good grades. Almost every science lecture had an accompanying PowerPoint, which was available online. During lecture, I would write notes in my notebook, excluding anything that was on the PowerPoint. If the professor said something I did not quite catch, I would write down as much as I could and circle it. After every lecture, I would open my notes, the PowerPoint, and the textbook and compile everything into one master Word document. I would write down everything I could not figure out on a separate sheet of paper. At least once a week, I would go to the office hours of the professor and go through all my questions with him/her, until I understood everything. While I was there, I also made a constant effort to get to know the professor. I would then go back to my Word document and perfect my notes. By the time the test was approaching, I had one large document consisting of everything I needed to know. I would copy and paste it into a new document and save it under stuff I need to study. I would then go through the new document and delete everything that I already knew. I was always surprised by how much I already knew just from creating this document. Anything I did not know or did not feel comfortable with, I would leave it on the document and write or draw out the concept on my mini whiteboard. I would then take this smaller document, copy and paste it into a new document, and run the procedure over again, until I felt comfortable with everything. I would then do the practice questions. Lastly, I would go back through the original document, making sure I still felt comfortable with everything. This procedure was essentially flawless; I graduated in seven semesters with a BS in biology, a minor in chemistry, and a 3.99 math/science GPA. Also, by the end of the semester, the professors really knew me and appreciated how much interest I had in the course. When it was time to ask for letters of recommendation, I had many great options.

Studying for the MCAT while being a full-time student is an overload on your brain. The MCAT covers so many subjects that the only way you can keep it all in your head at once is to rid yourself of other responsibilities. I tried studying for the MCAT while taking a full course load, and I did not do as well as I had hoped (32). It was also the most miserable four months of my life. If it is at all possible, you should try to complete your MCAT-related courses by the end of the first summer session after sophomore year. You should then dedicate about two months of your life to studying for the MCAT full-time and take it just before the beginning of junior year or early in the fall of your junior year. This is not an option for most people. My sister is planning on completing her MCAT-related courses by December of her junior year. For her spring semester of junior year, she is doing a study abroad program that does not start until the end of January. This gives her about a seven-week gap between semesters that she can dedicate entirely to MCAT studying, allowing her to take the exam just before going abroad. She is also going to start studying casually during the fall of her junior year to get a head start. If you have to study for the MCAT while taking classes or working, do not give up hope; it can be done.

Regardless of when you start studying for the MCAT, I cannot pretend to offer a one-size-fits-all study procedure for it. You need to decide what works best for you. Some people need to be part of an organized course to keep them on track, while others can study entirely on their own. I did a combination of the two. The only great advice I can give is to take as many practice exams as possible. AAMC sells old tests online, and you should definitely take all of those throughout your study period to track your progress and get used to thinking under pressure for the entire five-hour period. Other companies also sell practice tests. I think the more tests you take, the better. Also, Examkrackers sells books that have practice questions for each subject. These were the hardest questions I could find, so I think they helped a lot, especially when I needed to focus on one specific area. The MCAT is definitely the peak of the premed mountain. At some points, I did not know if I was going to make it to the top, but after I completed it, I could see the finish line, and the rest of the process was all downhill.

Every March, *US News & World Report* ranks all the medical schools according to a number of categories. The MSAR book is also released around that time, and it provides great information about each school. These sources can help you decide which schools to apply to. You should apply to a range of schools from reaches to backups. Your list will likely change when you get your MCAT scores back. I applied to every school in Florida to ensure that I would at least get into one school. At the end of the day, the goal is to get into any medical school; where you go is just icing. My parents are both foreign medical graduates, and both got the residency programs they wanted: plastic surgery and dermatology. You just need to get in somewhere.

The reason you should take your MCAT by April or May is that it takes five weeks to get the scores back, and you do not want to submit your primary applications until you know your scores. Most medical schools have a rolling admissions process, so the earlier you submit your applications, the better off you are. I know a premed adviser who tells her students who are thinking of applying in August to wait until the next year because they have missed their opportunity. The chances of getting accepted drop off sharply the longer you wait. The primary applications open in early May. You want to start working on those as soon as possible. You also want to get the writers of your letters of recommendation all the necessary information they need to submit them to AMCAS on time. After meticulously editing your primary application for weeks, you should be ready to submit it in an instant as early as you are allowed to (early June).

I very strongly recommend doing medical service work or research the summer after your junior year. Many secondary applications will ask you to share experiences that you did not write about on your primary application. In my case, I had pretty much shared all the significant experiences in my entire life in my primary application, so I needed to have new experiences to write about in my secondary applications. While you are waiting for secondary applications, your interview preparation should be going full speed. I remember studying for my interviews between seeing patients in the medical clinics in the Dominican Republic the June after my junior year.

Most schools give you months to return your secondary applications, but you should try to submit them as soon as possible for two reasons. The schools assume that the more time it takes you to respond, the less excited you are about attending their school. Also, it is rolling admissions, so you want your application as high up in the pile as possible. As soon as I got a secondary application, I would drop everything, lock myself in a room, work on it for hours, have a few people help me edit it, proofread it, and send it in as soon as possible. The most common secondary application question is "Why do you want to go to this school?" If at all possible, I would first write about my connection to the location of the school. I would then use the MSAR to find specific details about the school that interested me. I tended to focus on research, service opportunities, and curriculum. This is also a common interview question, so you can see one of my sample answers to it above (215). You should save a copy of every secondary essay that you write in a folder. You will find that many of your paragraphs and sentences can be used to answer different questions with only slight alterations. Your answers to secondary application questions and interview questions are both stemming from the same experiences, so feel free to mix and match excerpts between your secondary essay folder and your interview question document. I added all of my secondary essay questions to my interview question list too.

If you are waitlisted by a few schools, and one of them is your top choice, you should send an email to that school guaranteeing that you will go if you are accepted. Admissions people talk to each other; only send this email to one school. Also, if you have anything to add to your application after you send it in, you should update all of your schools about it, especially the schools that waitlisted you.

The premed process is a marathon, not a sprint. Just remember, it will all be worth it!

53759687R00056

Made in the USA
Lexington, KY
18 July 2016